C·L·A·S·S·I·C·A·L

Monologues *for* Women

MONOLOGUES FROM 16TH, 17TH, AND 18TH CENTURY PLAYS

EDITED BY KYLE DONNELLY

HEINEMANN · PORTSMOUTH, NH

Heinemann
A Division of Reed Publishing (USA) Inc.
361 Hanover Street, Portsmouth, NH 03801-3912
Offices and agents throughout the world

Offices and agents throughout the world

Library of Congress Cataloging-in-Publication Data

Classical monologues for women: monologues from 16th, 17th, and
    18th century plays / edited by Kyle Donnelly.
        p. cm.
    Includes bibliographical references.
    ISBN 0-435-08620-0 : $7.95
        1. English drama--Early modern and Elizabethan, 1500–1600.
    2. English drama--17th century. 3. English drama--18th century.
    4. Women--Drama. 5. Monologues. 6. Acting. I. Donnelly, Kyle.
    PR1245.C474 1992
    822'.04508'0082--dc20   92-29026
                                                                 CIP

Interior and cover design by Tom Allen, Pear Graphic Design
Printed in the United States of America
93 94 95 96 9 8 7 6 5 4 3 2

Table of Contents

Introduction xi

Serious

Abdelazer, or, The Moor's Revenge.....................................3
 Aphra Behn

Adventure of Five Hours 5
 Sir Samuel Tuke

The Adventures of Five Hours 9
 Sir Samuel Tuke

All Mistaken 11
 James Howard

The Changeling...12
 Thomas Middleton and William Rowley

The Constant Couple...14
 George Farquhar

The Constant Couple 15
 George Farquhar

The Destruction of Jerusalem, Part I 17
 John Crowne

The Destruction of Jerusalem, Part I 19
 John Crowne

Don Sebastian 21
 John Dryden

The Example...22
 James Shirley

The Fair Penitent 24
 Nicholas Rowe

Fatal Curiosity 26
    George Lillo

Gallathea...27
    John Lyly

The Guardian 29
    Abraham Cowley

King Henry V, or, The Conquest of France.......................30
    Aaron Hill

King Henry V, or, The Conquest of France.......................31
    Aaron Hill

The Libertine 32
    Thomas Shadwell

The London Merchant...34
    George Lillo

The Lost Lady...36
    William Barclay

The Mourning Bride..39
    William Congreve

A New Way To Pay Old Debts 41
    Philip Massinger

Perkin Warbeck...43
    John Ford

The Rebellion 45
    Thomas Rawlins

The Relapse 46
    Sir John Vanbrugh

The Rover..48
    Aphra Behn

The Rover..49
    Aphra Behn

The Sack of Rome..50
  Mercy Otis Warren

The Sack of Rome 51
  Mercy Otis Warren

The Sack of Rome..52
  Mercy Otis Warren

She Would and She Would Not...53
  Colley Cibber

Tis Pity She's A Whore...54
  John Ford

The Two Noble Kinsmen..56
  William Shakespeare and John Fletcher

The Two Noble Kinsmen..58
  William Shakespeare and John Fletcher

The Two Noble Kinsmen..60
  William Shakespeare and John Fletcher

The White Devil...61
  John Webster

The Witch of Edmonton..62
  John Dekker

Comic

All Mistaken..65
  James Howard

All Mistaken..66
  James Howard

The Beaux Stratagem 68
  George Farquhar

The Country Wife...70
  William Wycherly

The Double Dealer 72
  William Congreve

The Distress'd Wife...74
  John Gay

The Dutch Courtesan..76
  John Marston

The Dutch Courtesan..77
  John Marston

The Dutch Courtesan..79
  John Marston

Hyde Park..80
  James Shirley

I'll Tell You What 81
  Elizabeth Inchbald

Madam Fickle 83
  Thomas Durfey

The Man of Mode 84
  George Etherege

The Obstinate Lady 86
  Sir Aston Cokain

Polly Honeycombe...87
  George Colman

The Provoked Wife..89
  Sir John Vanbrugh

The Rivals 90
  Richard Brinsley Sheridan

The Rivals 91
  Richard Brinsley Sheridan

The Rivals...92
  Richard Brinsley Sheridan

The Rover 93
  Aphra Behn

Three Weeks After Marriage 94
  Samuel Foote

The Way To Keep Him..96
  Arthur Murphy

The Way To Keep Him..98
  Arthur Murphy

The Way of the World 100
  William Congreve

Serio-Comic

The Conscious Lovers..103
  Richard Steele

The Constant Couple...104
  George Farquhar

The Contrast 105
  Royall Tyler

Cutter of Coleman Street 107
  Abraham Cowley

Fatal Curiosity..109
  George Lillo

Fatal Curiosity 110
  George Lillo

Love Tricks 111
  James Shirley

The Maid's Revenge 112
  James Shirley

The New Inn 114
  Ben Jonson

The Obstinate Lady 116
    Sir Aston Cokain

The Obstinate Lady 117
    Sir Aston Cokain

The Obstinate Lady 119
    Sir Aston Cokain

The Projectors 120
    John Wilson

The Roaring Girl 122
    Thomas Dekker and Thomas Middleton

The Roaring Girl 123
    Thomas Dekker & Thomas Middleton

The Silent Woman, or Epicoene 125
    Ben Jonson

Bibliography...127

Introduction

I COULDN'T BEGIN TO COUNT the times actors have come up to me and asked, Do you know any good classical monologues that would be right for me? Finding a good monologue, in any category, is a tricky proposition. Finding one that is not seen repeatedly at auditions is quite difficult. Most theatres, if they've scheduled Shakespeare in their season, or if they regularly do classical or verse plays, want a "classical monologue" as part of their general auditions. Just what is considered a classical monologue? Most actors use, and rightly so, Shakespeare as their classical source. All actors who are interested in pursuing classical work should have a few good Shakespearean monologues under their belt. If you truly have a passion for Rosalind, or Helena, or Queen Margaret, you must, by all means, study these roles. With any luck, someday you'll get the chance to do more than audition with their monologues.

But directors are primarily interested in seeing and hearing how you handle verse and elevated language. Does it have to be Shakespeare? I think not. There are some exciting and challenging alternatives.

The wonderful, wide-ranging body of dramatic literature from the sixteenth, seventeenth, and eighteenth centuries is neglected by most American actors. Unfortunately, it is neglected by most theatrical producers as well. Hence, our exposure to this body of work is limited, except, perhaps in certain academic institutions. A notable exception is the Royal Shakespeare Company and their productions at the Swan Theatre in Stratford. Since 1986, the RSC at Stratford has been, as they state in their programs, "dedicated to the discovery and rediscovery of Shakespeare's context: plays by his contemporaries, plays that influenced him, plays that he influenced, and plays that he was rumored to have had a hand in writing." The RSC has helped bring attention to texts that had lapsed into obscurity. I have had the pleasure of directing two such plays, *The Rover,* by Aphra Behn, at the Goodman Theatre in Chicago, and *Hyde Park,* by James Shirley, at the Huntington Theatre in Boston. I discovered them to be eminently playable and delightful audience-pleasers. I urge you to open yourself up to these unfamiliar works.

This volume of women's monologues includes characters of all types and ages, confronting and wrestling with the social and political mores of the periods represented. Chastity and "reputation" were genuine concerns. Lady Peregrine in *The Example,* and Diana in *Gallathea* worry about potential shame and infamy; Maria in *The Contrast* expresses her concern for her reputation, "which is the life of a woman." Others, of course, worry less and allow themselves to be enraptured by the circumstances and sweet words of love. There is Mrs. Pinchwife, as she pens her innocent letter to Mr. Horner in *The Country Wife,* Milesia, with her touching tale of love in *The Lost Lady,* and the Queen in *Abdelazar,* who comes to the bitter awareness of a woman who has loved and lost. And, happily for the comediennes among us, some women are not above being silly in love, as the well-read Polly Honeycombe so aptly demonstrates with her insistence that life resemble a romance novel (a view shared by Lydia Languish in *The Rivals),* or Crispinella does with her description of the unsavory ceremony of kissing in *The Dutch Courtesan.*

There are Shakespearean echoes in some of the more serious females: Cleanthe (like Juliet) contemplates suicide in *The Obstinate Lady,* and the French Princess protests her proposed slavery to buy peace between England and France in *King Henry V, or, The Conquest of France.*

Most extraordinary are the women who express the unpopular position of unhappiness in marriage and dissatisfaction with their gender's lot in life. Selina flies from marriage in *Love Tricks,* while Lady Brute knows whereof she speaks when she denounces the institution. Millimant brilliantly proposes her conditions for marriage to Mirabell in *The Way of the World;* Mrs. Carol in Hyde Park claims she will have none of it. Perhaps most extraordinary of all are the early feminist preachings of Mrs. Godsgood in *The Projectors,* as she proposes a "She Senate" to offer advice and counsel to the men's governing body.

So you will find much to choose from here, in both distinct characterization and specific point of view. The range of age, period, and style, allows every actor to find a suitable monologue. If done well, these pieces will let you demonstrate a facility with complicated language, a sense of style, and an adventurous spirit. And directors, especially those looking for classical actors, will be delighted to have something "new" to watch and listen to.

But a director wants more than originality of material. Particularly with this kind of material, your most important considerations will be clarity of text and confident individual interpretation. First, of course, you must understand the text thoroughly and speak it clearly, being sure to allow the poetic element in the writing to soar. Ultimately, however, your individual interpretation is critical to the success of your audition. These plays, especially the comedies, center around the characters. Although there are plot twists galore, it is the individuality of the character against a backdrop of intrigue or drama that makes the play touching or humorous. The character names give you an idea of both the specificity and the broad bold strokes used by the playwright in depicting the characters themselves—Lady Willit, Mrs. Godsgood, Lady Plyant, Lady Brute. But it is the actor who can bring her individuality to the characterization who will create a living, breathing character, rather than a museum piece.

What practical steps can you take to handle these unfamiliar and not always easily understandable texts? First, and most importantly, you must *read the play.* You cannot hope to create a complete, complex character if you do not know the context of the monologue. It has been said many times before, and cannot be said enough: Read the play. Consult the bibliography at the back of the volume, and then go to your local university library. You should be able to find many, if not all, of these plays there.

Next, it is important to acknowledge the difficulty of understanding the text on a first reading. The plots are often quite complicated, and the language, both usage and structure, can be quite unfamiliar. I have often had to read these plays many times, keeping one finger on the character breakdown, in order to keep straight who's who, who's doing what, and who wants to do what with (or to) whom. So don't feel mentally deficient if it takes you extra time and effort to get it.

The third important step in working on these monologues is to understand what you are saying. This sounds obvious, but it is a basic problem and often one an actor neglects in her initial work on the text. When in doubt at all about context, go back to the original play. Look up unfamiliar words, preferably in an Oxford English Dictionary, which gives original references and ancient definitions. Look up familiar words if they're used in an unfamiliar context. You may discover something about that word you never knew before. If a passage is particularly complicated, try breaking the sentences down grammatically. Most importantly, don't assume or generalize. The more specific your meaning, the clearer and more interesting your characterization — and the moments that build it — will be, both for you and for your audience.

Fourth, change what doesn't work for you. A monologue must be able to stand on its own, apart from the play. We have chosen beginnings, middles, and ends of speeches; in some cases, we've cut and pieced several speeches together. If you find that beginning or ending your monologue of choice in a different spot, or making a few internal cuts works better for you, more power to you. The versions here are certainly not set in stone. You might also change a piece by taking out obscure references, or changing extremely difficult or obtuse words that sound strange to modern ears. However, be careful not to sanitize the work. Even though your audience may not know exactly what a reference means, the sound of the words may convey a particular tone or specific sensibility. And don't forget that it is part of the actor's art to be able to convey a context that will give a word meaning.

After choosing a piece, doing your homework, and getting it up on its feet, consider a test run for your monologue. Try it out on someone who has not been privy to any of your process, not necessarily for formal criticism, but for feedback on the clarity and effectiveness of your work. Did she understand what you were saying? Did he get a sense of the character without knowing the play or the period? Were you believable? Getting the reaction of someone you trust may help you clarify sections you have inadvertently skimmed over or neglected.

Auditioning is rarely easy, but give yourself credit for choosing a classical audition piece not seen by every director hundreds of times. I can only speak for myself, but as a director who has sat through many an audition, good and bad, I certainly appreciate the change of pace.

Kyle Donnelly

Serious

Abdelazer, or, The Moor's Revenge

Aphra Behn   Act I, scene i; Serious

Queen: My gentle Abdelazer, 'tis thy Queen,
  Who has laid aside the Business of her state,
  To wanton in the kinder Joys of Love—
  Play all your sweetest Notes, such as inspire
  The active soul with new and soft Desire,
  Whilst we from eyes, thus dying, fan the fire . . .
  Can ought that I command displease my Moor?
  Why dost thou frown? To whom was that curse sent?
  To me? It cannot be. To me, sweet Moor?
  No, no, it cannot—prithee smile upon me—
  Smile, whilst a thousand Cupids shall descend
  And call thee Jove, and wait upon thy smiles,
  Deck thy smooth brow with flowers;
  Whilst in my eyes, needing no other Glass,
  Thou shalt behold and wonder at thy Beauty . . .
  Where has thou learnt this language, that can say
  But those rude words? Away, away, be gone?
  Am I grown ugly now?
  Didst thou not love me once, and swore that Heav'n
  Dwelt in my face and eyes?
  Since all my passion, all my soft entreaties
  Can do no good upon thee,
  I'll see, since thou has banish'd all thy love,
  That love, to which I've sacrificed my honor,
  If thou hast any sense of gratitude,
  For all the mighty graces I have done thee.
  Ingrate!
  Have I for this abus'd the best of Men,
  My noble husband?
  Depriving him of all the joys of love,
  To bring them all entirely to thy bed;

3

Neglected all my vows, and sworn 'em here a-new,
Here, on thy lips—
Exhausted treasures that would purchase crowns,
To buy thy smiles—to buy a gentle look;
And when thou didst repay me—blest the Giver?
Oh, Abdelazer, more than this I've done—
This very hour, the last the King can live,
Urg'd by thy witchcraft, I his life betray'd.
And is it thus my bounties are repaid?
Whate'er a crime so great deserves from Heaven
By Abdelazer might have been forgiven:
But I will be revenged by penitence,
And e'er the king dies, own my black offense.

Camilla: Your story, I confess, is strangely moving;
    Yet if you could my fortune weigh with yours
    In scales of equal sensibility,
    You would not change your sufferings for mine.
    It is to open my wounds afresh, dear Porcia,
    But you must be obey'd.
    His excellence the Conde d'Oniate,
    Being sent an ambassador to the emperor,
    We, having the honor to be near allied
    To his lady, went with him. My brother
    Was desir'd by her to make that journey;
    Whose tenderness for me not suffering him
    To let me stay behind, I was engaged
    And treated by the ambassadress my cousin
    With more respect than I could ever merit.
    We had not pass'd much time in the
    Emperor's court
    When my dear brother unexpectedly
    By urgent business was called back to Seville.
    On our return (passing too near a garrison
    Of the enemy's) our convoy was surprised
    And routed by a party of their horse.
    We, being prisoners, were hurried straight away
    To the enemy's quarters, where my ill fate
    Made me appear too pleasing to the eyes
    Of their commander, who at first approach
    Pretends to parlay in a lover's style;
    Protesting that my face had changed our fortunes,
    And him my captive made; but finding soon
    How little he advanced in his design
    By flattery and his feigned submission,

He shifts his person, calls me his prisoner,
And swears my virgin treasure was his prize.
But yet he protests he had much rather owe it
To my indulgence than his own good-fortune.
And so, through storms and calms, the villain still
Pursues his course to his accursed end.
But finding me inflexible to his threats
As well as fawnings, he resolves to use
The last and uncontrolled argument
Of impious men in power—force.

*[Ending #1: There are three possible endings for this monologue.
Continue for longer monologue.]*

My brother, alas, was long before
Borne away from me in the first encounter;
Where having certainly behaved himself
As well became his nation and his name,
Remain'd sore wounded in another house.
The brute approaches, and by violence
Endeavors to accomplish his intent;
I invoke my guardian angel, and resist,
But with unequal force, though rage supplied
Those spirits which my fear had put to flight.
At length, grown faint with crying out and striving,
I spied a dagger by the villain's side
Which, snatching boldly out, as my last refuge,
With his own arms I wound the savage beast:
He at the stroke unseized me, and gave back.
So guilt produces cowardice. Then I,
The dagger pointing to my breast, cried out,
"Villain, keep off, for, if thou dost persist,
I'll be myself both sacrifice and priest:
I boldly now defy thy lust and hate;
She that dares choose to die, may brave her fate!"
Immediately, the drums and trumpets sound,

Pistols go off, and a great cry, "To Arms,
To arms!" The lustful satyr flies. I stand,
Fixed with amazement to the marble floor,
Holding my guardian dagger aloft,
As if the ravisher threatened still.

[Ending #2]

Freed from this fright, my spirits flowed so fast
To the forsaken channels of my heart,
That they, who by their orderly access
Would have supported life, by throngs oppress:
O'ercharged with joy, I fell into a swoon,
And that which happened during this interval
Is not within the circle of my knowledge.
At my return to life, opening my eyes,
Think, dearest Porcia, how I was astonish'd
To find there, kneeling by my side, a man
Of a most noble form, who, bowing to me:
"Madam," says he, "y'are welcome to the world;
Pardon, I pray, the boldness of a stranger
Who humbly sues you to continue in it.
Or, if you needs will leave us, stay at least
Until I have revenged your wrongs, and then
I'll wait upon you to the other world;
For, you withdrawn, this will a desert seem,
And life a torment."
'Twas so surprising, that my confusion
Checked my reply; but I suppose my looks
Did speak the grateful language of my heart;
For I perceived an air of joy enlighten
His manly face; but, O, how soon 'twas clouded
By fresh alarms! We heard the soldiers cry,
Where's Antonio? The enemy has rallied,
And coming up to give a second charge!
He started up, and with a mien that marked

The conflict 'twixt his honor and his love,
Madam, he says, the soul was never yet
With such convulsion from the body torn,
As I from you, but it must never be said
That Don Antonio de Mendoza
Follows those in danger whom he ought to lead.
Thus the vanquished conqueror disappeared,
Leaving that image stamped on my heart
To which I all the joys must sacrifice
Of the poor remnant of my wretched life;
If properly to live I may be said,
When all my hopes of seeing him are dead.
[Ending #3]

The Adventures of Five Hours

Sir Samuel Tuke   *Act I, scene ii; Serious*

Porcia: My heart is so oppressed with fear and grief
　　That it must break, unless it finds relief;
　　The man I love forced to fly my sight.
　　And like a Parthian, kills me in his flight:
　　One whom I never saw I must embrace,
　　Or else destroy the honor of my race;
　　A brother's care, more cruel than his hate:
　　O, how perplexed are the intrigues of fate.
　　You know, Camilla, best how generously
　　How long, and how discreetly, Don Octavio
　　Has serv'd me, and what trials of his faith
　　And fervour I did make, ere I allow'd him
　　The least hope to sustain his noble love.
　　Cousin, all this you know; twas in your house
　　We had our interviews, where you were pleased
　　To suffer feigned addresses to yourself
　　To cover from my watchful brother's eyes
　　The passion which Octavio had for me.
　　And how one evening (O, that fatal hour)
　　My brother, passing by Don Carlos' house
　　With his great friend and confidant, Don Pedro,
　　Did chance to see the unfortunate Octavio
　　In your balcony, entertaining me:
　　Whom not believing there he took for you,
　　My back being towards him, and both dressed alike.
　　Enraged with jealousy, this cruel man
　　(To whom all moderation is unknown)
　　Resolves to stamp all your neglects of him
　　In his supposed rival, poor Octavio's, heart.
　　They take their stand i'th'corner of our street;
　　And after some little time Octavio,

Free from suspicion as design of ill,
Retires; they assault him, and in's own defense
He kills Don Pedro, and is forc'd to fly.
My brother cruelly pursues him still
With such insatiate thirst after revenge
That nothing but Octavio's blood can quench:
Covering his ill-nature and suspicion
With the resentment of Don Pedro's death. This brother
To whose impetuous will my deceased parents
(May their souls rest in peace!) having condemned
Me and my fortune, treats me like a slave:
So far from suffering me to make my choice
That he denounces death if I refuse;
And now, to frustrate all my hopes at once,
Has very lately made me sign a contract
To one in Flanders whom I never saw,
And is this night (they say) expected here.
Was every misery like mine, Camilla?
Reduc'd to such extremes, past all relief?
If I acquaint my brother with my love
To Octavio, the man whom he most hates,
I must expect the worst effect of fury:
If I endeavor to forget Octavio
Even that attempt renews his memory,
And heightens my disquiet: if I refuse
To marry, I am lost; if I obey,
I cast Octavio and myself away.
Two such extremes of ill no choice admit.
Each seems the worst: on which rock shall I split?
Since, if I marry, I cannot survive,
And not to marry were to die alive,
What can there be in nature more afflicting
Than to be torn from th'object of my love,
And forc'd t'embrace a man whom I must hate?

All Mistaken

James Howard   *Act I, scene i; Serious*

Amphelia: How has my tongue belied my too true heart,
In speaking hate unto the duke,
And love to Ortellus! I, hate the duke?
So eyes do sleep, that long have known no rest.
How could my lips give passage to such words
And not have clos'd forever?
Not by my heart's direction, I am sure; for that
So swell'd, being injured by my mouth, as, had
Not pride and reason kept it here from this
Unquiet feat, it would have forced a way
To Archimedes' breast, and there have whispered to
His heart my tongue's untruth. Why should I love
This man that shows me nothing but contempt
And hate? Rouse, drooping heart, and think
Of that. Think of it always, so by degrees
'Twill bring a winter round thee, that in time
Shall chill the heat of thy undone and lost
Affections. Oh, it is not true that all
Our sex love change; then might I find one path
That leads to it;
That womanish vice were virtue now in me,
'Twould free my heart and that were charity.
See where he comes again. Oh, how I love
And hate that man! Now, help me, pride, and fill
My breast with scorn; and prithee, tongue, take heed
You do not falter. Hear not, my heart, that will
Distract thy speech, and so betray my feigned
Unkindness.

The Changeling

Thomas Middleton and William Rowley Act IV, scene i; Serious

Beatrice-Joanna: This fellow has undone me endlessly.
Never was bride so fearfully distressed.
The more I think upon the ensuing night,
And whom I am to cope with in embraces,
One who's ennobled both in blood and mind,
So clear in understanding (that's my plague now),
Before whose judgment will my fault appear
Like malefactors' crimes before tribunals—
There is no hiding on't, the more I dive
Into my own distress. How a wise man
Stands for a great calamity! There's no venturing
Into his bed, what course soe'er I light upon,
Without my shame, which may grow up to danger;
He cannot but in justice strangle me
As I lie by him, as a cheater use me.
'Tis a precious craft to play with a false die
Before a cunning gamester. Here's his closet,
The key left in't, and he abroad i' the park:
Sure 'twas forgot; I'll be so bold as to look in't.
Bless me! A right physician's closet 'tis,
Set round with vials, every one her mark too.
Sure he does practice physic for his own use,
Which may be safely called your great man's wisdom.
What manuscript lies here? "The book of Experiment,
Call'd Secrets in Nature"; so 'tis, 'tis so;
"How to know whether a woman be with child or no."
I hope I am not yet; if he should try, though!
Let me see, folio forty-five. Here 'tis,
The leaf tucked down upon't, the place suspicious.
"If you would know whether a woman be with child or
not, give her two spoonfuls of the white water in glass C—"

Where's that glass C? Oh, yonder, I see't now—
"and if she be with child, she sleeps full twelve hours
after; if not, not."
None of that water comes into my belly.
I'll know you from a hundred; I could break you now,
Or turn you into milk, and so beguile
The master of the mystery, but I'll look to you.
Ha! That which is next is ten times worse:
"How to know whether a woman be a maid or not";
If that should be applied, what would become of me?
Belike he has a strong faith of my purity
That never yet made proof, but this he calls
"A merry sleight, but true experiment, the author
Antonio Mizaldus. Give the party you suspect
the quantity of a spoonful of water in the glass M, which
    upon her that
is a maid makes three several effects: 'twill make her
    incontinently
gape, then fall into a sudden sneezing, last into a violent
    laughing;
else dull, heavy, and lumpish." Where had I been? I fear it, yet
'tis seven hours to bedtime.

The Constant Couple

George Farquhar   *Act V, scene i; Serious*

Angelica: What madness, Sir Harry, what wild dream of loose
desire could prompt you to attempt this baseness? View me
well. The brightness of my mind, methinks, should lighten
outwards, and let you see your mistake in my behavior. I
think it shines with so much innocence in my face, that it
should dazzle all your vicious thoughts. Think now I am
defenseless, 'cause alone. Your very self is guard against yourself: I'm sure, there's something generous in your soul; my
words shall search it out, and eyes shall fire it for my own
defense. Behold me, sir; view me with a sober thought, free
from those fumes of wine that throw a mist before your sight,
and you shall find that every glance from my reproaching
eyes is arm'd with sharp resentment, and with a virtuous pride
that looks dishonor dead.

The Constant Couple

George Farquhar   *Act III, scene v; Serious*

Lady Lurewell: Leave trifling! 'Tis a subject that always sours my temper. But since, by the faithful service, I have some reason to confide in your secrecy, hear the strange relation. Some twelve years ago I lived at my father's house in Oxfordshire, blest with innocence, the ornamental but weak guard of blooming beauty. I was then just fifteen, an age oft fatal to the female sex: our youth is tempting, our innocence credulous, romances moving, love powerful, and men are—villains! Then it happened, that three young gentlemen, from the university, coming into the country, and being benighted and strangers, called at my father's house. He was very glad of their company, and offered them the entertainment of his house. They had some private frolic or design in their heads, as appeared by their not naming one another; which my father, perceiving, out of civility, made no inquiry into their affairs. Two of them had a heavy, pedantic, university air, a sort of disagreeable scholastic boorishness in their behavior; but the third! He was, but, in short, nature cut him out for my undoing! He seemed to be about eighteen. He had a genteel sweetness in his face, a graceful comeliness in his person, and his tongue was fit to soothe soft innocence to ruin. His looks were witty, and his expressive eyes spoke softer, prettier things, than words could frame. His discourse was directed to my father, but his looks to me. After supper, I went to my chamber and read Cassandra; then went to bed and dreamt of him all night; rose in the morning, and made verses: so fell desperately in love. My father was well pleased with his conversation, that he begged their company next day; they consented; and next night, he bribed my maid, with his gold, out of her honesty; and me, with his rhetoric, out of my honor. She admitted him to my chamber, and there he vowed, and

15

swore, and wept, and sighed—and conquered. He swore that he would come down from Oxford in a fortnight and marry me. Alas! What wit had innocence like mine? He told me that he was under an obligation to his companions of concealing himself then, but that he would write to me in two days, and let me know his name and quality. After all the binding oaths of constancy, joining hands, exchanging hearts, I gave him a ring with this motto, "Love and Honor." Then we parted; but I never saw the dear deceiver more. I need not tell my griefs, which my father's death made a fair pretense for; for he left me sole heiress and executrix to three thousand pounds a year. At last, my love for this single dissembler turned to a hatred of the whole sex, and, resolving to divert my melancholy, and make my large fortune subservient to my pleasure and revenge, I went to travel, where, in most Courts of Europe, I have done some execution. Here I will play my last scene; then retire to my country house, live solitary, and die a penitent.

The Destruction of Jerusalem, Part I

John Crowne   *Act II, scene ii; Serious*

Queen Berenice: Let the soft sleep to dying lovers go,
And on despairing minds her balm bestow.
The joy the happy hour's approaching near,
When I must leave my dull devotion here,
 And on love's wings to my Vespasian fly,
Transports my soul to such an ecstasy
That with an empire's price should not be bought
The single pleasure of one flying thought.
Tell me, Semandra, dost thou not espy
A new delightful spirit in my eye?
Does not my cheerful blood its revels take,
And often in my cheeks fresh sallies make? . . .
Begone! Thou paintest me in a flattering dress. . . .
Indeed, my glass will needs obliging be,
I fear th'unfaithful thing takes part with thee.
Nay, I confess I'm pleas'd: for I must own
I was half weary of devotion grown,
What with the grief for my dear brother's blood,
What with the clamors of the foolish crowd,
Who their own safety madly will oppose:
What with impatience too at length to close
These even long weeks of grave devotion here,
Which did to me a tedious age appear,
I was so tir'd—that now the time is gone,
Methinks my eyes another air put on;
And lay their penitential looks aside,
With all the joy of a young, smiling bride . . .

*[The next section could be used as a separate monologue, or could
continue from the first part as one long monologue.]*

'Twas on a great triumphant day at Rome,
When all the adoration gods assume,
Or flattering priests ascribe to powers divine,
When with uncommon flames their altárs shine,
Was to the young victorious Titus paid,
When he through Rome a pompous entry made.
It were too dull and tedious to display
The bright and various splendors of that day,
Young Titus' fame ne'er spoke him half so fair;
Men gaz'd with envy, women with despair.
We who, the King our father lately dead,
By rebels chas'd, to Rome's protection fled,
I felt my heart a secret flame possess,
But thought my eyes secur'd my heart success.
Tho Roman ladies did my rank contemn,
At least my beauty might contend wit them.
And so it prov'd; for the whole time he stayed,
His sole address was at my altars made:
Which they resented with such scorn, and pride,
Some rag'd with madness, some with envy died.
But, oh my stars! how pleas'd was I to see
My beauty thus revenge my quality!

The Destruction of Jerusalem, Part I

John Crowne   *Act IV; Serious—Good*

Queen Berenice: And am I thrown into the rebels' power,
And must I never see Vespasian more?
It cannot be decreed! I rave, I rave!
Nature no warning at our parting gave!
The air would sure have sigh'd, the caves have moan'd.
The clouds have wept, the hollow mountains groan'd;
All friends of love would have exprest their fear
Of two so kind, so constant, and so dear:
Nature would then have had convulsive pains
And blood would have startled out from both our veins . . .
I came not here to offer you a peace,
The Roman power and glory to increase;
To add to empire was not my design
Though I may hope one day it will be mine;
All my ambitions do no higher rise
Than at a smile from my Vespasian's eyes.
But 'twas from him all danger to remove—
Danger, the mighty rival to my love—
Danger, that does enjoy him more than I,
To whom from me he every hour does fly;
Leaps to her arms, and I'm afraid one day
The harpy will devour the glorious prey.
In camp how do I pass the day in frights,
In horrid dreams and broken sleep the nights?
With my own cries myself I often wake,
And waking, joy to find out my mistake.
Then in a sound and pleasing sleep I fall
But in the morning for my lord I call:
How does my lord? to every one I cry,
If any look with a dejected eye;
But sad or pale, for no reply I stay,

Conclude my lord is slain, and faint away.
What do the wounded and the dying do?
Love joins in one what are in nature two.
The breasts of lovers but one soul contain,
Which equally imparts delight or pain.
Once he on danger did too strongly press—
For he has all great virtues to excess;
In gallant things endures no mean degree,
But loves and fights still in extremity;
When, oh! he wounded did return from fight—
You may conceive th'effect of such a sight.
My sorrows' violence no tongue can tell,
Thrice in my women's arms all cold I fell;
And only was to wretched life again
Tormented, by the throbbing of his pain.
Hourly I watch'd by him both night and day,
And never mov'd, but when I swoon'd away.
My eye forever fixt on him I kept,
Nor lost the sight of him, but when I wept;
In all his pains I groan'd, his fevers burn'd,
Nor found I health or ease till his return'd.

Don Sebastian

John Dryden   *Act II, scene i; Serious*

Almeyda: You turn my prison to a paradise;
   But I have turn'd your empire to a prison:
   In all your wars, good fortune flew before you;
   Sublime you sat in triumph on her wheel,
   Till in my fatal cause your sword was drawn;
   The weight of my misfortunes dragged you down.
   Leave then the luggage of your fate behind,
   To make your flight more easy, leave Almeyda.
   Nor think me left a base ignoble prey
   Expos'd to this inhuman tyrant's lust:
   My virtue is a guard beyond my strength,
   And death, my last defense, within my call.
   If shunning ill be good, then death is good
   To those who cannot shun it but by death:
   Divines but peep on undiscovered Worlds,
   And draw the distant landscape as they please:
   But who has e'er returned from those bright regions
   To tell their manners and relate their laws?
   I'll venture landing on that happy shore
   With an unsully'd body, and white mind;
   If I have err'd, some kind inhabitant
   Will pity a strayed soul, and take me home.
   What joys can you possess or can I give
   Where groans of death succeed the sighs of love?
   Our Hymen has not on his saffron robe;
   But muffled up in mourning, downward holds
   His drooping torch, extinguish'd with his tears.

The Example

James Shirley   *Act III, scene i; Serious*

Lady Peregrine: Enough, too much.
 My Lord, I hop'd when last
 Your importunity inforc'd my promise
 Of other answer, I should never see you,
 If being a sad prisoner to my chamber
 Might have prevented your access; but since
 I am betrayed to this discourse, receive
 What the necessity of fate compels to:
 Not your estate,
 Though multiplied to kingdoms, and those wasted
 With your invention, to serve my pleasures,
 Have power to bribe my life away from him,
 To whose use I am bid to wear it; be yet just,
 And seek no further to pollute the stream
 Of my chaste thoughts; I'll rather choose to die
 Poor wife to Peregrine, than live a King's
 Inglorious strumpet; can you think, my Lord,
 Should I give up my freedom to your bent
 And for the pride of wealth, sell woman in me,
 (For she must lose that name that once turns whore)
 Could I arrive at impudence enough
 To come abroad, and not be mov'd to hear
 My shame from every tongue, but scorn my infamy,
 (As tis the nature of this sin to strengthen
 Itself still with a greater) could you think,
 If no religion can correct your wildness,

Another's price, or pleasure, would not buy me
Even from your arms? There is no faith in lust,
And she that dares be false to one she loves,
Will twine with all the world, and never blush for't,
Kiss, and betray as often. Think on this,
And call your self home.

The Fair Penitent

Nicholas Rowe   *Act V; Serious*

Calista: 'Tis well! These solemn sounds, this pomp of horror
   Are fit to feed the frenzy in my soul;
   Here's room for meditation, ev'n to madness,
   Till the mind burst with thinking; this dull flame
   Sleeps in the socket; sure the book was left
   To tell me something—for instruction, then—
   He teaches holy sorrow and contrition,
   And penitence;—is it become an art, then?
   A trick that lazy, dull, luxurious gown-men
   Can teach us to do over? I'll no more on't.
     [Throws the book away]
   I have more real anguish in my heart
   Than all their pedant discipline e'er knew.
   What charnel has been rifl'd for these bones?
   Fie! this is pageantry;—they look uncouthly,
   But what of that, if he or she that owned them
   Safe from disquiet sit and smile to see
   The farce their miserable relics play?
   But here's a sight is terrible indeed;
   Is this that haughty, gallant, gay Lothario?
   That dear, perfidious—Ah! how pale he looks!
   How grim with clotted blood, and those dead eyes!
   Ascend ye ghosts, fantastic forms of night,
   In all your diff'rent dreadful shapes ascend,
   And match the present horror, if you can . . .

[Continue for longer monologue]

It is Sciolto! Be thyself, my soul;
Be strong to bear his fatal indignation,
That he may see thou art not lost so far
But somewhat still of his great spirit lives
In the forlorn Calista—Happy were it I had died,
And never lost that name of daughter
 .... My soul was rudely drawn from yours,
A poor, imperfect copy of my father
Where goodness and the strength of manly virtue
Was thinly planted, and the idle void
Filled up with light belief and easy fondness;
It was because I loved, and was a woman.
I have turned my eyes inward upon myself
Where foul offense and shame have laid all waste;
Therefore my soul abhors the wretched dwelling,
And longs to find some better place of rest.

Fatal Curiosity

George Lillo   Act I, scene ii; Serious

Charlot: Methought I sat, in a dark winter's night,
  My garments thin, my head and bosom bare,
  On the wide summit of a barren mountain,
  Defenseless and exposed in that high region
  To all the cruel rigors of the season.
  The sharp, bleak winds pierced through my shiv'ring frame,
  And storms of hail and sleet and driving rains
  Beat with impetuous fury on my head,
  Drenched my chilled limbs, and poured a deluge round me.
  On one hand ever-gentle Patience sat,
  On whose calm bosom I reclined my head,
  And on the other, silent Contemplation.
  At length to my unclosed and watchful eyes,
  That long had rolled in darkness and oft raised
  Their cheerless orbs towards the starless sky
  And sought for light in vain, the dawn appeared.
  And I beheld a man, an utter stranger
  But of a graceful and exalted mien
  Who pressed with eager transport to embrace me.
  I shunned his arms, but at some words he spoke,
  Which I have now forgot, I turned again,
  But he was gone, and oh, transporting sight!
  Your son, my dearest Wilmot, filled his place!
    . . . But what's to come,
  Though more obscure, is terrible indeed.
  Methought we parted soon, and when I sought him,
  You and his father—yes, you both were there—
  Strove to conceal him from me. I pursued
  You with my cries, and called on Heaven and earth
  to judge my wrongs and force you to reveal
  Where you had hid my love, my life, my Wilmot!

Gallathea

John Lyly   *Act III, scene iv; Serious*

Diana: Now, ladies, doth not that make your cheeks blush that
makes mine ears glow, or can you remember without sobs
that which Diana cannot think upon without sighs? What
greater dishonor could happen to Diana, or to her nymphs
same, than that there can be any time so idle that should
make their heads so addle? Your chaste hearts, my nymphs,
should resemble the onyx, which is hottest when it is whitest,
and your thoughts, the more they are assaulted with desires,
the less they should be affected. You should think love like
Homer's moly, a white leaf and a black root, a fair show and a
bitter taste. Of all trees the cedar is greatest and hath the
smallest seeds; of all affections love hath the greatest name
and the least virtue. Shall it be said, and shall Venus say it,
nay, shall it be seen, and shall wantons see it, that Diana, the
goddess of chastity, whose thoughts are always answerable to
her vows, whose eyes never glanced on desire, and whose
heart abateth the point of Cupid's arrows, shall have her virgins to become unchaste in desires, immoderate in affection,
intemperate in love, in foolish love, in base love? Eagles cast
their evil feathers in the sun, but you cast your best desires
upon a shadows. The birds lose their sweetness when they
lose their sights, and virgins all their virtues with their
unchaste thoughts. Unchaste Diana calleth that that hath
either any show or suspicion of lightness. Oh, my dear
nymphs, if you knew how loving thoughts stain lovely faces,
you would be as careful to have the one as unspotted as the
other beautiful.

Love's desire corrupteth all other virtues. I blush, ladies,
that you, having been heretofore patient of labors, should not
become prentices to idleness, and use the pen for sonnets, not

the needle for samplers. And how is your love placed? Upon pelting boys, perhaps base of birth, without doubt weak of discretion. Ay, but they are fair. Oh, ladies, do your eyes begin to love colors, whose hearts were wont to loath them? Is Diana's chase become Venus' court, and are your holy vows turned to hollow thoughts? Foolish girls, how willing you are to follow that which you should fly. And thou shalt see, Cupid, that I will show myself to be Diana, that is, conqueror of thy loose and untamed appetites. Did thy mother, Venus, under the color of a nymph send thee hither to wound my nymphs? Doth she add craft to her malice, and, mistrusting her deity, practice deceit? Is there no place but my groves, no persons but my nymphs? Cruel and unkind Venus, that spiteth only chastity, thou shalt see that Diana's power shall revenge thy policy and tame this pride. As for thee, Cupid, I will break thy bow and burn thine arrows, bind thy hands, clip thy wings, and fetter thy feet. Venus' rods are made of roses, Diana's of briars. Let Venus, that great goddess, ransom Cupid, that little god. These ladies here whom thou hast infected with foolish love shall both tread on thee and triumph over thee. Thine own arrow shall be shot into thine own bosom, and thou shalt be enamored not on Psyches, but on Circes. I will teach thee what it is to displease Diana, distress her nymphs, or disturb her game.

The Guardian

Abraham Cowley   *Act IV, scene i; Serious*

Lucia: Every thing now has left me; tears themselves,
   The riches of my very grief, forsake me:
   Sorrow, methinks, shews nakedly without 'em.
   My sighs are spent, too; and my wearied lungs
   Deny me fresh supplies: and I appear
   Like some dull melancholy April-even,
   When after many a shower the heav'ns still lowre
   As if they threatened more; and the fled Sun
   Leaves nothing but a doubtful blush behind him.
   And I could wish my eternal night were coming,
   Did I but know who 'tis that makes me wish it:
   Else, when my soul is ready for her flight,
   And knows not who it is she must forgive,
   A thousand light suspicions will call
   Her charity several ways; and I may chance
   To doubt thee, Truman. But thou art abus'd:
   I know not why; but sure thou coulds't not do it.
   I fear thee, Cousin. When we were both girls,
   Thou wouldst accuse me falsely to my Mistress,
   And laugh to see my tears. I fear thee, Cousin;
   But I'll not judge too rashly: for I would not
   Have any innocent wrong'd as I have been.
   But I'm resolv'd to try her. She's now seeking
   (Hoping that all my fortunes now are hers)
   For a new maid t'attend her. That maid I'll be.
   Clothes I have got already; and my face
   Grief has disguis'd: that and my voice some art
   Will quickly alter. I have left a note
   Upon my chamber window, which will keep 'em
   From all suspicions of my staying here.

King Henry V, or, The Conquest of France

Aaron Hill   Act II, scene ii; Serious

Princess: No, no, my Charlot! I disdain the motive;
 Love is a flame too bright, too clear, to burn
 As interest bids it—What imports it me,
 That coward France can shake at sudden danger?
 What are my father's fears to my affections?
 Shall I, because this hot brain'd King of England
 Sweeps o'er our land with war and devastation,
 Shall I, for that, grow fond of the destroyer?
 Smile at the waste of his unpunish'd insolence,
 Throw myself headlong into hostile arms,
 And sell my peace of mind to save my country?
 Rather shall death possess me, than this Harry! . . .
 Am I, because they call my father Sovereign
 To be the slave, the property of France?
 Can nothing buy their peace, but my undoing?
 How nobler were it to quell rage with fury!
 In arms to check the bold invader's pride,
 Meet storm with storm, and buckle in a whirlwind!
 Then, if the dire event swept me away,
 My ruin, tho' 'twere dreadful, would be glorious:
 But to hold out a proffer of my person,
 Poorly, and at a distance! Hang me out,
 Like a shook flag of truce!—Oh, 'tis a meanness
 That shames ambition, and makes pride look pale!
 Where is the boasted strength of manhood, now?
 Sooner than stoop to this, were mine the scepter,
 I would turn Amazon;—my softness hid
 In glittering steel, and my plum'd helmet nodding
 With terrible adornment, I would meet
 This Henry with a flame more fierce than love.

King Henry V, or, The Conquest of France

Aaron Hill   *Act II, scene ii; Serious*

Princess: You, brother, may content yourself with that;
But I brook not so well the shame design'd me;
I am, on both sides, then, the toy of state!
One king's condition, and the other's engine!
The tool which Harry's treason is to work with!
Whence shall I borrow rage to speak my anger?
And every fury that can lash assist me!
What will my peaceful father say to this?
Yes! He has chosen nobly for his daughter!
Charles has a generous son-in-law in Harry:
O France! What lazy frost has chill'd your blood?
Where is that pride of arms, that boasted courage,
Which your vain tongues are swell'd with?
Where's the soul
That, in the warlike Gauls, your glorious ancestors,
Shook the proud world, and sham'd the Roman Caesars?
If there remains the shadow of your past glory,
If any spark yet glimmers in your breasts,
Of your once furious fire, go, down upon him;
Scatter his army like the wind-drive sands,
Seize him alive, and bring him me a prisoner.

The Libertine

Thomas Shadwell   *Act II; Serious*

Maria [in man's habit]: Thus have I abandoned all my Fortune,
    and laid by my sex,
Revenge for thee. Assist me now,
You instruments of blood, for my dear brothers,
And for my much more dear Octavio's sake.
Where are my bravos?
O let them show no more remorse
Than hungry lions oer their prey will.
How miserable am I made by that
Inhumane monster! No savage beast,
Wild deserts e'er brought forth, provoked
By all its hungers, and its natural rage,
Could yet have been so cruel.
Oh, my Octavio! Whither thou art fled
From the most loving and most wretched
Creature of her sex? What ages of delight
Each hour with thee brought forth?
How much, when I had thee, was all the world
Unenvied by me! Nay, I pitied all my sex
That could have nothing worth their care
Since all the treasure of Mankind was mine.
Methought I could look down on queens, when he
Was with me; but now, compared to me,
How happy is the wretched, whose sinews
Crack upon the merciless Engine
Of his torture? I live with greater torments than he dies.
Now, my just grief to just revenge give place.
I am ashamed of these soft tears. Till I've
Revenged thy horrid murder, oh that I could
Make the villain linger out an age in
Torments! But I will revel in his blood: Oh,

I could suck the last drop that warms the
Monster's heart, that might inspire me with
Such cruelty as vile Man, with all his horrid
Arts of power, is yet a stranger to.
Then I might root out all his cursed race.
Thou are my dear and faithful creature;
Let not thy Fortunes thus be wrack'd with mine.
Be gone, and leave thy most unhappy mistress;
One that has miseries enough to sink the sex.
Oh, that I had been some poor lost Mountain girl,
Nurs'd up by goats, or suck'd by wild beasts,
Exposed to all the rage of heats and killing colds.
I ne'er could have been abandoned to such fury.
More savage cruelty reigns in cities,
Then ever yet in deserts among the
Most venomous serpents, and remorseless
Ravenous beasts, could once be found.
So much has barbarous Art debauched
Man's innocent nature.
    'Tis blood I now must spill or
Lose my own in the attempt. But if I can
Have the fortune, with my own hand, to reach
The dog's vile heart, I then shall die
Contented, and in the other world I'll
torture him so, devils shall learn of me to
use the damned.
Come on. So just a cause would turn the
Vilest ruffian to a saint.

The London Merchant

George Lillo   *Act IV, scene xvii; Serious*

Millwood: Men of all degrees and all professions I have known,
yet found no difference but in their several capacities. All
were alike wicked to the utmost of their power. In pride, con-
tention, avarice, cruelty, and revenge the reverent priesthood
were my unerring guides. From suburb-magistrates, who live
by ruined reputations, as the unhospitable natives of
Cornwall do by shipwrecks, I learned that to charge my innocent neighbors with crimes was to merit their protection, for
to screen the guilty is the less scandalous when many are suspected, and detraction, like darkness and death, blackens all
objects and levels all distinction. Such are your venal magis-
trates who favor none but such as, by their office, they are
sworn to punish. With them, not to be guilty is the worst of
crimes, and large fees, privately paid, is every needful virtue
. . . I hate you all, and expect no mercy—nay, I ask for none.
I have done nothing that I am sorry for. I followed my incli-
nations, and that the best of you does every day. All actions
are alike natural and indifferent to man and beast who
devour or are devoured as they meet with others weaker or
stronger than themselves . . . . I am not fool enough to be an
atheist, though I have known enough of men's hypocrisy to
make a thousand simple women so. Whatever religion is in
itself, as practiced by mankind it has caused evils you say it
was designed to cure. War, plague, and famine has not
destroyed so many of the human race as this pretended piety
has done, and with such barbarous cruelty as if the only way
to honor Heaven were to turn the present world into Hell
. . . . What are your laws, of which you make your boats, but
the fool's wisdom and the coward's valor, the instrument and
screen of all your villanies by which you punish in others
what you act yourselves or would have acted, had you been in

their circumstances? The judge who condemns the poor man for being a thief had been a thief himself, had he been poor. Thus, you go on deceiving and being deceived, harassing, plaguing, and destroying one another, but women are your universal prey.

Women, by whom you are, the source of joy,
With cruel arts you labor to destroy.
A thousand ways you our ruin pursue,
Yet blame in us those arts first taught by you.
Oh, may, from hence, each violated maid
By flatt'ring, faithless, barb'rous man betray'd,
When robb'd of innocence and virgin fame,
From your destruction raise a nobler name:
To right their sex's wrongs devote their mind,
And future Millwoods prove, to plague mankind!

The Lost Lady

William Barclay   *Act V, scene i; Serious*

Milesia: My dear friend, you shall know all my story.
  'Tis true, my uncle did design my death
  For loving Lysicles; for, at his coming hither,
  He charg'd me, by all ties that were between us,
  To hate him as the ruin of his honor;
  And yet, for some dark end I understood not,
  Resolv'd to leave me here. I swore obedience,
  But knew not what offense it was to keep
  An oath so made, till I had seen Lysicles,
  Which at your house I did, when he came wounded
  From hunting of the boar. All but his name
  Appear'd most godlike to me. You all did run
  To stop his wounds, and I thought I might see
  My enemy's blood; yet soon did pity seize me,
  To see him bleed. Thus, love taking the shape
  Of pity, glided unseen of me into my heart,
  And whilst I thought myself but charitable,
  I nurs'd my infant love with milk of pity,
  Till he grew strong enough to take me prisoner.
  I found his eyes on mine, and ere I could
  Remove them, heard him say, he'd thank his fortune
  For this last wound, it 'twere the cause
  Of seeing me; then took his leave,
  But left me speechless that I could not say,
  My heart, farewell! After this visit our loves
  Grew to that height that you have heard of.

[Ending #1]

I had a servant unsuspected of me
(For none I trusted that observ'd our meetings,)

Who guessing by my sighs that love had made them,
Betray'd them to my uncle. On Pallas' eve
He rush'd into my chamber, his sword drawn,
And snatch'd me by the arm. I fell down,
But, knowing yet no fault, could beg no pardon.
Awhile our eyes did only speak our thoughts;
At length out of his bosom he pull'd a paper:
It was the contract betwixt my lord and me;
And ask'd me if I would avow the hand.
Heaven, said I, has approv'd it, and the gods
Have chose this way to reunite our houses.
Stain of thy kindred's honor, he exclaims,
"Was there no other man to ease your lust
But he that was our greatest enemy?
Resolve to die: thy blood shall hide the stains
Of our dishonor,"
Leaving me oppress'd with sighs
And tears, yet not of sorrow and repentance,
But fear that I should leave my dearest servant,
Commands his cruel slaves to murder me
As I descended; and lest pity should
Create remorse in their obdurate hearts,
The lights were put out. Then hastily
my name was heard. I then entreated her
That betray'd me to tell them I was coming,
And took this time to write unto my lord.
She went, but by the way was seized
And strangled by those murderers
That expected me. My uncle heard
Her latest groans; and now the act was pass'd
His power to help, he wish'd it were undone:
Brings lights to see the body, and perceiv'd
The strange mistake. By signs and lifted eyes
Confess'd heaven's hand was in't; yet would not leave
His revenge here—commands his slaves to change
My clothes with hers was slain; then takes the head off,

And on the trunk did leave a note which told
My death for living Lysicles, in hope my ruin,
Knowing his noble nature, would be his.
At midnight, quits this town, leaving none behind
Were conscious of the fact—immures me in his house,
    till I escap'd in that disguise
I wore when I first came to you.
At my arrival here,
I heard my Lysicles should marry you,
And therefore kept the habit I was in,
To search unknown the truth of this report,
And practis'd in the private actions
Of some near friends, got an opinion
I could presage the future. Thus was I
Sought by you, thus I found the faith
Of my dear Lysicles, when at the tomb I did
Appear his ghost, and had reveal'd myself, had not
The shame of doubting such a faith kept my desires in.

[Ending #2]

The Mourning Bride

William Congreve   *Act III, scene i; Serious*

Zara: What, does my face displease thee,
  That having seen it, thou dost turn thy eyes
  Away, as from deformity and horror?
  If so, this sable curtain shall again
  Be drawn, and I will stand before thee seeing
  And unseen. Is it my love? ask again
  That question, speak again in that soft voice,
  And look again, with wishes in thy eyes.
  O no, thou canst not, for thou seest me now
  As she, whose savage breast has been the cause
  Of these thy wrongs; as she, whose barbarous rage
  Has loaded thee with chains and galling irons:
  Well, dost thou scorn me, and upbraid my falseness;
  Could one that lov'd thus torture what she lov'd?
  No, no, it must be hatred, dire revenge,
  And detestation, that could use thee thus.
  So thou dost think; then, do but tell me so;
  Tell me, and thou shall see how I'll revenge
  Thee on this false one, how I'll stab and tear
  This heart of flint, 'til it shall bleed, and thou
  Shalt weep for mine, forgetting thy own miseries . . .
  O, Heav'n! My fears interpret
  This thy silence; somewhat of high concern,
  Long-fashioning within thy laboring mind,
  And now just ripe for birth, my rage has ruin'd.
  Have I done this? Tell me, am I so curs'd?
  Swift as occasion, I
  My self will fly, and earlier than the morn,
  Wake thee to freedom. Now, 'tis late; and yet
  Some news, few minutes past arriv'd, which seem'd
  To shake the temper of the King—Who knows

What racking cares disease a monarch's bed?
Or love, that late at night still lights his camp
And strikes his rays through dusk, and folded lids,
Forbidding rest; may stretch his eyes awake.
Thou canst not owe me more, not have I more
To give, than I've already lost. But as
The present Form of our engagement rests,
Thou hast the Wrong, 'till I redeem thee hence;
That done, I leave thy justice to return
My love. Adieu.

A New Way To Pay Old Debts

Philip Massinger   *Act IV, scene i; Serious*

Lady Alworth: I ne'er pressed, my lord,
  On other's privacies, yet against my will,
  Walking, for health sake, in the gallery
  Adjoining to your lodgings, I was made
  (So vehement and loud he was) partaker
  Of his tempting offers.
  'Tis, my lord, a woman's counsel,
  But true, and hearty; wait in the next room,
  But be within call; yet not so near to force me
  To whisper my intents.
  Now, my good lord, if I may use my freedom
  As to an honored friend—
  I dare then say thus:
  As you are noble (howe'er common men
  Make sordid wealth the object and sole end
  Of their industrious aims) twill not agree
  With those of eminent blood (who are engag'd
  More to prefer their honors, than to increase
  The state left to 'em by their ancestors)
  To study large additions to their fortunes
  And quite neglect their births: though I must grant
  Riches well got to be a useful servant,
  But a bad master.
  As all wrongs, though thrust into one scale
  Slide of themselves off, when right fills the other,
  And cannot bide the trial, so all wealth
  (I mean if ill acquired), cemented to your honor
  By virtuous ways achiev'd, and bravely purchas'd,
  Is but as rubbish pour'd into a river
  (Howe'er intended to make good the bank)
  Rend'ring the water that was pure before

Polluted, and unwholesome. I allow
The heir of Sir Giles Overreach, Margaret,
A maid well qualified, and the richest match
Our north part can make boast of, yet she cannot
With all that she brings with her, fill·their mouths
That will never forget who was her father;
Or that my husband Alworth's lands, and Welbourne's
(How wrung from both needs no repetition)
Were real motive, that more work'd your lordship
To join your families, than her form, and virtues;
You may conceive the rest.

Perkin Warbeck

Katherine: It is decreed, and we must yield to fate,
   Whose angry justice, though it threaten ruin,
   Contempt, and poverty, is all but trial
   Of a weak woman's constancy in suffering.
   Here in a stranger's and an enemy's land,
   Forsaken and unfurnished of all hopes
   But such as wait on misery, I range
   To meet affliction wheresoe'er I tread.
   My train and pomp of servants is reduced
   To one kind gentlewoman and this groom.
   Sweet Jane, now whither must we?
      Home! I have none.
   Fly thou to Scotland; thou has friends will weep
   For joy to bid thee welcome; but, O Jane,
   My Jane, my friends are desperate of comfort,
   As I must be of them; the common charity,
   Good people's alms and prayers of the gentle,
   Is the revenue must support my state.
   As for my native country, since it once
   Saw me a princess in the height of greatness
   My birth allowed me, here I make a vow
   Scotland shall never see me being fallen
   Or lessened in my fortunes. Never, Jane,
   Never to Scotland will I more return.
   Could I be England's queen—a glory, Jane,
   I never fawned on—yet the king who gave me
   Hath sent me with my husband from his presence,
   Delivered us suspected to my husband's nation,
   Rendered us spectacles to time and pity.
   And is it fit I should return to such
   As only listen for our descent

From happiness enjoyed to misery
Expected, though uncertain? Never, never!
Alas, why dost thou weep, and that poor creature
Wipe his wet cheeks too? Let me feel alone
Extremities, who know to give them harbor;
Nor thou nor he has cause. You may live safely.

The Rebellion

Thomas Rawlins

Aurelia: Oft have I heard my brother with
    Proud of the office praise this lovely lor
    And my trapped soul did with as eager
    Draw in the breath; and now, o Aurelia!
    Buried with him must all the joy thou hast
    Forever sleep; and with a pale consumption,
    Pitying him, wilt thou thyself be ruined?
    He must not die; if there be any way
    Reveal'd to the distressed, I will find it.
    Assist a poor lost virgin, some good power,
    And lead her to a path, whose secret tract
    May guide both him and me unto our safety.
    Be kind, good wits, I never until now
    Put you to any trouble; 'tis your office
    To help at need this little world you live by;
    Not yet! O, dullness, do not make me mad—
    I have't, blessed brains! Now shall a woman's wit
    Wrestle with fate, and if my plot but hit,
    Come off with wreaths. My duty, nay, my all,
    I must forsake, lest my Antonio fall.

manda: Would the world were on fire, and you in the
    middle on't.
Begone; leave me.
At last I am convinced. My eyes are testimonies
of his falsehood. The base, ungrateful, perjured villain.
Good gods, what slippery stuff are men composed of?
Sure the account of their creation's false
And 'twas the woman's rib they were formed of.
But why am I thus angry?
This poor relapse should only move my scorn.
'Tis true, the roving flights of his unfinished youth
Had strong excuses from the plea of nature;
Reason had thrown the reins loose on his neck
And slipt him to unlimited desire.
If therefore he went wrong, he had a claim
To my forgiveness, and I did him right.
But since the years of manhood rein him in,
And reason well digested into thought
Has pointed out the course he ought to run,
If now he strays,
'Twould be as weak and mean in me to pardon
As it has been in him t'offend.
But hold:
'Tis an ill cause, indeed, where nothing's to be said for't.
My beauty possibly is in the wane;
Perhaps sixteen has greater charms for him.
Yes, there's the secret. But let him know,
My quiver's not entirely emptied yet:
I still have darts and I can shoot 'em too,
They're not so blunt but they can enter still,
The want's not in my power, but in my will.

46

Virtue's his friend, or, through another's heart
I yet could find the way to make him smart.

The Rover

Aphra Behn   *scene xix; Serious*

Angellica: You said you loved me.
And at that instant, I gave you my heart.
I'd pride enough and love enough to think
That it could raise thy soul above th vulgar,
Nay, make you all soul, too, and soft and constant.
Why did you lie and cheapen me? Alas,
I thought all men were born to be my slaves
And wore my power like lightning in my eyes;
But when love held the mirror, that cruel glass →
Reflected all the weakness of my soul;
My pride was turned to a submissive passion
And so I bowed, which I ne'er did before
To anyone or anything but Heaven.
I thought that I had won you, and that you
Would value me the higher for my folly.
But now I see you gave me no more than dog lust,
Made me your spaniel-bitch; and so I fell
Like a long-worshiped idol at the last
Perceived a fraud, a cheat, a bauble. Why
Didst thou destroy my too long fancied power?
Why didst thou give me oaths? Why didst thou kneel
And make me soft? Why, why, didst thou enslave me?

The Rover

Aphra Behn   *scene x; Serious*

Lucetta: This gold will buy us things. Alas, I curse my future that has made me a slave to Sancho, since I was sold. Would I had coin enough to fly to England and try my fortune as the colonel did. But what base means we girls o' the galleys must submit to, ere we can gain our ends. A common whore; oh, fie; one that must yield to all beastly embraces, yea, all the nasty devices men's lust can invent; nay, not only obey but blow the fire, too, and hazard all diseases when their lust commands. And so sometimes we are enjoyed aforetimes, but never after. And yet I cannot but laugh at this English fool. If I cannot rise in this bad world, yet 'tis some recompense to bring such a fellow down. O, now is this bull calf as naked as I was once on shipboard, and now I pity him. There's for thee, poor Essex calf.

The Sack of Rome

Mercy Otis Warren   *Act IV, scene ii; Serious*

Edoxia: Where shall I fly? to what sequestered shade
   Where the world's distant din no more alarms,
   Or warring passions burst through natures tie
   And make mankind creation's a foulest stain.
   Horror and guilt stare wild in every eye;
   Freedom extinguished in the flames of lust
   Bleeds fresh beside Rome's long expiring fame;
   Virtue's become the rude barbarian's jest,
   Bartered for gold, and floating down the tide
   Of foreign vice, stained with domestic guilt!
   Oh, could I hide in some dark hermitage
   Beneath some hollow, dismal, broken cliff,
   I'd weep forlorn the miseries of Rome
   Till time's last hollow broke, and left me quiet
   On the naked strange. Ah! Leo,
   Durst thou be still the friend of sad Edoxia?
   Hast thou the courage yet to visit grief,
   And sooth a wretch by sympathetic tears
   And reconcile me to the name of man?
   Canst show me one less cruel than the tiger
   Nursed in the wilds and feasting on the flesh
   Of all but his own species?
   This predilection's left to man alone,
   To drink and riot on his brother's blood.

The Sack of Rome

Mercy Otis Warren   *Act IV, scene ii; Serious*

Edoxia: Mock not my woe, Insult not my distress.
   What is Rome to me? I have no country.
   What's life, or empire, or the world to me?
   And art thou come to sue for Maximus?
   Whose blackened soul, blown up by fierce ambition
   Assumes the reins and drives the courser on,
   With furious passion and unbridled list?
   Remember, Leo,
   The blood that flowed from Poplicola's veins
   From breast to breast through Horatian line,
   And thence to me convey'd—a generous stream
   That animates and warms Edoxia's heart,
   Shall ne'er be tainted by a base submission.
   Tell him I'm not the coward fool he thinks,
   That guilty greatness has no charms for grief;
   I scorn his impious passion—detest his name.
   Tell him, a traitor's heart, though swelled
   By adulation's base perfume, has not a hand
   To wield the imperial scepter.
   My former friend, the guardian of my youth;
   I thought thy soul cast in a purer mould,
   Above the servile line, not thus to court
   And meanly grovel, for a tyrant's smile.
   Leave me, base wretch—go fawn on thy new master.
   Tell him at once, Edoxia dares to die.

The Sack of Rome

Mercy Otis Warren   Act IV, scene ii; Serious

Edoxia: Thy venerable grief, my aged friend
   Softens resentment, which thy zeal inflamed.
   In that kind tear, the soul of Leo shines;
   Yet say, is Rome so poor and abject grown,
   So far debased that when a ruffian dares
   To stab his prince, and boldly challenge
   To his impious bed the wife of his
   Assassinated lord—none dare oppose?
   Has Rome for this so often fought and conquered?
   Has the best blood the Roman name can boast
   Reddened the Tiber with its purple streams,
   To purchase freedom by the swift perdition
   Of every bold invader, from Tarquin's reign,
   To the more fatal day, when guilty Maximus
   Assumed the purple? May thunders roll,
   And streams irruptive, blast a wretch like him,
   Or sheets of livid flame enwrap Edoxia
   From his hated sight.
   Go on, and bear this answer to thy lord.
   Thou great first cause, who bids the tempest rage,
   And rends with mighty peals the darkened air,
   Light up the skies and blaze from north to south,
   Thy vengeance pour on complicated guilt.

She Would and She Would Not

Colley Cibber   *Act IV; Serious*

Hypolita: [In men's attire] Nay, then, sir—Mercy, Mercy! [She throws herself at his feet]. And since I must confess, have pity on my youth, have pity on my love! Unless your generous compassion spares me, I am sure the most wretched youth that ever felt the pangs and torments of successless passion. I confess, my fortune's much inferior to my pretenses in this Lady, though indeed I'm born a gentleman, and bating this attempt against you, which even the last extremities or a ruin'd love have forced me to, ne'er yet was guilty of a deed or thought that could debase my birth. But if you knew the torments I have born from her disdainful pride, the anxious days, the long watched winter nights I have endured to gain of her perhaps at last a cold relentless look, indeed, you'd pity me. My heart was so entirely subdued, the more she slighted me, the more I lov'd; and as my pains increased, grew farther from cure. Her beauty struck me with that submissive awe, that when I dar'd to speak my words and looks were softer than an Infant's blushes; yet all the pangs of my persisting passion still were vain; nor showers of tears, nor storms of sighs, could melt or move the frozen hardness of her dead compassion. But yet so subtle is the flame of love, spite of her cruelty, I nourished still a secret living hope, till hearing, sir, at last she was designed your bride, despair compelled me to this bold attempt of personating you; Her father knew not me, or my unhappy love; I knew too you ne'er had seen her face, and therefore hop'd, when I should offer to repair with twice the worth of value, sir, I robbed you of, begging thus low for your forgiveness. I say, I hoped at least your generous heart, if ever it was touched like mine, would pity my distress, and pardon the necessitated wrong.

'Tis Pity She's A Whore

John Ford   *Act V, scene i; Serious*

Annabella: Pleasure, farewell, and all ye thriftless minutes
   Wherein false joys have spun a weary life.
   To these my fortunes now I take my leave.
   Thou, precious Time, that swiftly rid'st in post
   Over the world, to finish up the race
   Of my last fate, here stay thy restless course,
   And bear to ages that are yet unborn
   A wretched, woeful woman's tragedy.
   My conscience now stands up against my lust
   With despositions charactered in guild,
   And tells me I am lost; now I confess
   Beauty that clothes the outside of the face
   Is cursed if it be not clothed with grace.
   Here, like a turtle, mewed up in a cage,
   Unmated, I converse with air and walls,
   And descant on my vile unhappiness.
   O Giovanni, that has had the spoil
   Of thine own virtues and my modest fame,
   Would thou hadst been less subject to those stars
   That luckless reigned at my nativity;
   Oh, would the scourge due to my black offense
   Might pass from thee, that I alone might feel
   The torments of an uncontrolled flame . . .
      That man, that
   Blessed friar,
   Who joined in ceremonial knot my hand
   To him whose wife I now am, told me oft
   I trod the path to death, and showed me how.
   But they who sleep in lethargies of lust
   Hug their confusion, making heaven unjust,
   And so did I.

[Ending #1]

Forgive me, my good genius, and this once
Be helpful to my ends. Let some good man
Pass this way, to whose trust I may commit
This paper double lined with tears and blood:
Which, being granted, here I sadly vow
Repentance, and a leaving of that life
I long have died in. . . .

[Ending #2]

   Here, holy man—
Commend me to my brother; give him that,
That letter; bid him read it and repent.
Tell him that I, imprisoned in my chamber,
Barred of all company, even of a guardian,
Who gives me cause of much suspect, have time
To blush at what hath passed; bid him be wise,
And not believe the friendship of my lord.
I fear much more than I can speak; good father,
The place is dangerous, and spies are busy;
I must break off—you'll do't?
Thanks to the heavens, who have prolonged my breath
To this good use. Now I can welcome death.

[Ending #3]

The Two Noble Kinsmen

William Shakespeare and John Fletcher

Act III, scene iii; Serious

Jailer's Daughter: 'Tis now well nigh morning.
  No matter; would it were perpetual night,
  And darkness lord o' th' world. Hark; 'tis but a wolf!
  In me hath grief slain fear, and but for one thing
  I care for nothing, and that's Palamon.
  I reck not if the wolves would jaw me, so
  He had this file; what if I hallowed for him?
  I cannot hallow; if I whooped, what then?
  If he not answered, I should call a wolf,
  And do him but that service. I have heard
  Strange howls this livelong night; why may't not be
  They have made prey of him? He has no weapons;
  He cannot run; the jingling of his gyves
  Might call fell things to listen, who have in them
  A sense to know a man unarmed, and can
  Smell where resistance is. I'll set it down
  He's torn to pieces; they howled many together,
  And then they fed on him; so much for that.
  Be bold to ring the bell. How stand I then?
  All's charred when he is gone. No, no, I lie;
  My father's to be hanged for his escape,
  Myself to beg, if I prized life so much
  As to deny my act; but that I would not,
  Should I try death by the dozens. I am moped;
  Food took I none these two days; sipped some water.
  I have not closed mine eyes,
  Save when my lids scoured off their brine.
  Alas, Dissolve, my life; let not my sense unsettle,
  Lest I should drown, or stab, or hang myself.
  O state of nature, fail together in me,

Since thy best props are warped! So, which way now?
The best way is the next way to a grave;
Each errant step beside is torment. Lo,
The moon is down, the crickets chirp, the screech owl
Calls in the dawn. All offices are done,
Save what I fail in; but the point is this,
An end, and that is all.

The Two Noble Kinsmen

William Shakespeare and John Fletcher   Act II, scene ii; Serious

Jailer's Daughter: Why should I love this gentleman? 'Tis odds
    He will never affect me; I am base,
    My father the mean keeper of his prison,
    And he a prince. To marry him is hopeless;
    To be his whore is witless. Out upon't!
    What pushes are we wenches driven to
    When fifteen once has found us! First I saw him;
    I, seeing, thought he was a goodly man;
    He has as much to please a woman in him—
    If he please to bestow it so—as ever
    These eyes yet looked on. Next I pitied him,
    And so would any young wench, o' my conscience,
    That ever dreamed, or vowed her maidenhead
    To a young, handsome man. Then I loved him,
    Extremely loved him, infinitely loved him;
    And yet he had a cousin, fair as he, too;
    But in my heart was Palamon, and there,
    Lord, a what a coil he keeps! To hear him
    Sing in an evening, what a heaven it is!
    And yet his songs are sad ones. Fairer spoken
    Was never gentleman; when I come in
    To bring him water in a morning, first
    He bows his noble body, then salutes me, thus:
    'Fair, gentle maid, good morrow; may thy goodness
    Get thee a happy husband.' Once he kissed me;
    I loved my lips the better ten days after—
    Would he would do so every day! He grieves much,
    And me as much to see his misery.
    What should I do to make him know I love him?
    For I would fain enjoy him. Say I ventured
    To set him free? What says the law then? Thus much

For the law, or kindred! I will do it;
And this night, or tomorrow, he shall love me.

The Two Noble Kinsmen

William Shakespeare and John Fletcher Act III, scene iv; Serious

Jailer's Daughter: I am very cold, and all the stars are out, too,
The little stars and all, that look like aglets.
The sun has seen my folly. Palamon!
Alas, no; he's in heaven. Where am I now?
Yonder's the sea, and there's a ship; how't tumbles!
And there's a rock lies watching under water;
Now, now, it beats upon it; now, now, now,
There's a leak spring, a sound one; how they cry!
Spoon her before the wind, you'll lose all else;
Up with a course or two, and tack about, boys.
Good night, good night, you're gone. I am very hungry.
Would I could find a fine frog; he would tell me
News from all parts o'th'world; then would I make
A carrack of a cockleshell, and sail
By east and north-east to the King of the Pygmies,
For he tells fortunes rarely. Now my father,
Twenty to one, is trussed up in a trice
Tomorrow morning; I'll never say a word.

The White Devil

John Webster *Act IV, scene ii; Serious*

Vittoria: No matter.
   I'll live so now I'll make the world recant
   And change her speeches. You did name the Duchess.
   Whose death God revenge
   On thee, most godless Duke.
   What have I gained by thee but infamy?
   Thou hast stained the spotless honor of my house,
   And frighted thence noble society:
   Like those, which sick o' the palsy, and retain
   Ill-scenting foxes 'bout them, are still shunn'd
   By those of choicer nostrils.
   What do you call this house?
   Is this your palace? Did not the judge style it
   A house of penitent whores? Who sent me to it?
   Who hath the honor to advance Vittoria
   To this incontinent college? Is't not you?
   Is't not your high preferment? Go, but brag
   How many ladies you have undone, like me.
   Fare you well, sir. Let me hear no more of you.
   I had a limb corrupted to an ulcer,
   But I have cut it off: and now I'll go
   Weeping to heaven on crutches.
   For your gifts, I will return them all, and I do wish
   That I could make you full executor
   To all my sins. O that I could toss myself
   Into a grave as quickly: for all thou are worth
   I'll not shed one tear more;—I'll burst first.

The Witch of Edmonton

John Dekker   *Act I, scene i; Serious*

Mother Sawyer: Still wrong'd by every slave, and not a dog
Bark in his dame's defense? I am call'd witch,
Yet am myself bewitched from doing harm.
Have I given up myself to thy black lust
Thus to be scorn'd? Not see me in three days?
I'm lost without my Tomalin. Prithee, come;
Revenge to me is sweeter far than life.
Thou art my raven, on whose coal-black wings
Revenge comes flying to me. O my best love!
I am on fire, even in the midst of ice,
Raking my blood up till my shrunk knees feel
Thy curl'd head leaning on them. Come then, my darling;
If in the air thou hover'st, fall upon me
In some dark cloud; and, as I oft have seen
Dragons and serpents in the elements,
Appear thou now so to me. Art thou i' the sea?
Muster up all the monsters from the deep,
And be the ugliest of them, so that my bulch
Show but his swarth cheek to me, let earth cleave
And break from Hell, I care not. Could I run
Like a swift powder mine beneath the world,
Up would I blow it all, to find out thee,
Thou I lay ruin'd in it.

Comic

All Mistaken

James Howard   *Act II; Comic*

Mirida: I'll lay my head, ne'er a girl in Christendom
  Of my age can say what I can: I'm now
  But five years i'th' teens, and I have fool'd
  Five several men. My humor
  Is to love no man, but to have as many
  Love me as they please, come cut or long tail.
  'Tis a rare diversion, to see what several
  Ways my flock of lovers have in being
  Ridiculous. Some of them sigh so damnably
  That 'tis as troublesome as a windy day.
  There's two of them that make their love together,
  By languishing eye-casts; one of them has
  One eye bigger than the other, and looks like a tumbler;
  And that eye's like a musket
  Bullet, and I expect every minute when he
  Will hit me with it, he aims so right at me.
  My other lover looks asquint, and to
  See him cast languishing eyes would make a
  Woman with child miscarry. There is also
  A very fat man, Master Pinguister, and
  A very lean man that loves me. I tell the
  Fat man I cannot marry him till he's
  Leaner, and the lean man I cannot marry
  Him till he's fat. So one of them purges
  And runs heats every morning, to pull down
  His sides, and th'other makes his tailor stuff
  His clothes to make him show fatter. O, what
  Pleasure do I take in fooling of mankind!

All Mistaken

James Howard   *Act V; Comic*

Mirida: Hold, sir. I forbid the banns. I'd
   Rather hear a long sermon than
   Hear a parson ask me: Mirida,
   Will you have this man for your
   Wedded husband, to have and to hold,
   From this day forward, for better for worse
   In sickness or in health and so forth.
   Ay, and perhaps after we have been
   Married half a year, one's
   Husband falls into a deep consumption,
   And will not do one the favor to
   Die neither, then we must be
   Ever feeding him with caudles.
   Oh, from a husband with consumption
   Deliver me. And think how weary I should be
   Of thee, Philidor, when once we were
   Chain'd together: the very name of
   Wife would be a vomit to me; then
   nothing but "Where's my wife? Call
   My wife to dinner, call my wife to supper;"
   And then at night, "Come wife, will you
   Go to bed?" That would be so troublesome,
   To be call'd by one's husband every night
   To go to bed. Oh, that dull, dull,
   Name of husband. If you please, sir, never propose
   Marrying to us, till both of us have
   committed such faults as are death
   By the law; then, instead of
   Hanging us, marry us.

And then you shall hear how
Earnestly we shall petition
Your highness to be hang'd rather than
Married.

The Beaux' Stratagem

George Farquhar   *Act II, scene i; Comic*

Mrs. Sullen: Country pleasures! Racks and torments! Dost think, child, that my limbs were made for leaping of ditches, and clambering over stiles? Or that my parents, wisely forseeing my future happiness in country pleasures, had early instructed me in rural accomplishments of drinking fat ale, playing at whisk, and smoking tobacco with my husband? Or of spreading plasters, brewing of diet-drinks, and stilling rosemary-water, with the good old gentlewoman, my mother-in-law? Not that I disapprove rural pleasures, as the poets have painted them; in their landscape, every Phyllis has her Corydon, every murmuring stream, and every flowery mead, gives fresh alarms to love. Besides, you'll find, that their couples were never married. But yonder I see my Corydon, and a sweet swain it is, Heaven knows! Come, Dorinda, don't be angry; he's my husband, and your brother, and, between both, is he not a sad brute? O, sister, sister! If ever you marry, beware of a sullen, silent sot, one that's always musing, but never thinks. There's some diversion in a talking blockhead; and since a woman must wear chains, I would have the pleasure of hearing 'em rattle a little. Now you shall see, but take this by the way. He came home this morning at his usual hour of four, wakened me out of a sweet dream of something else, by tumbling over the tea-table, which he broke all to pieces; after his man and he had rolled about the room, like sick passengers in a storm, he comes flounce into bed, dead as a salmon into a fishmonger's basket; his feet cold as ice, his breath hot as a furnace, and his hands and his face as greasy as his flannel night-cap. O matrimony! He tosses up the clothes with a barbarous swing over his shoulders, disorders the whole economy of my bed, leaves me half-naked, and my whole night's comfort is the tuneable serenade of that wakeful nightingale, his nose! Oh, the pleasure of counting the melancholy clock by a snoring husband! But now, sister, you shall see how handsomely, being a well bred gentleman, he will beg my pardon.

The Country Wife

William Wycherly   *Act IV, scene ii; Comic*

Mrs. Pinchwife: For Mr. Horner—So, I am glad he has told me his name; Dear Mr. Horner, but why should I send thee such a letter, that will vex thee, and make thee angry with me?—well, I will not send it—Ay, but then my husband will kill me—for I see plainly, he won't let me love Mr. Horner— but what care I for my husband—I won't, so I won't send poor Mr. Horner such a letter—but then my husband—But oh—what if I writ at bottom, my husband made me write it—Ay, but then my husband would see't. Can one have no shift? Ah, a London woman would have had a hundred presently; stay—what if I should write a letter, and wrap it up like this, and write upon't too. Ay, but then my husband would see't. I don't know what to do—But yet y vads, I'll try, so I will—for I will not send this letter to poor Mr. Horner, come what will on't.

Dear, Sweet, Mr. Horner—So—[She writes, and repeats what she hath writ] my husband would have me send you a base, rude, unmannerly letter—but I won't—so—and would have me forbid you loving me—but I won't—so—and would have me say to you, I hate you poor Mr. Horner—but I won't tell a lie for him—there—for I'm sure if you and I were in the country at cards together—m so—I could not help treading on your toe under the table—so—or rubbing knees with you, and staring in your face, 'till you saw me—very well—and then looking down, and blushing for an hour together—so— but I must make haste before my husband come; and now he has taught me to write letters; you shall have longer ones from me, who am

    Dear, dear, poor dear Mr. Horner, your most
    Humble Friend and Servant to command
    'til death, Margery Pinchwife.

Stay, I must give him a hint at bottom—so—wrap it up just like t'other—so—now write, For Mr. Horner. But oh now what shall I do with it? for here comes my husband.

The Double Dealer

William Congreve   *Act II; Comic*

Lady Plyant: Oh, such a thing! The impiety of it startled me—
to wrong so good, so fair a creature, and one that loved you
tenderly—'tis a barbarity of barbarities, and nothing could be
guilty of it . . . Why, gads my life, cousin Mellefont, you cannot be so peremptory as to deny it, when I tax you with it to
your face; for now Sir Paul's gone, you are corum nobis . . . .
Fiddle-faddle, don't tell me of this and that, and everything in
the world, but give me mathemacular demonstration, answer
me directly—but I have not patience—oh! The impiety of it,
as I was saying, and the unparalleled wickedness! Oh merciful
Father! How could you think to reverse nature so, to make
the daughter the means of procuring the mother? Ay, for
though I am not Cynthia's own mother, I am her father's
wife, and that's near enough to make it incest. Oh, reflect
upon the horror of that, and then the guilt of deceiving
everybody; marrying the daughter, only to make a cuckold of
the father; and then seducing me, debauching my purity, and
perverting me from the road of virtue, in which I have trod
thus long, and never made one trip, not one faux pas; oh,
consider it, what would you have to answer for, if you should
provoke me to frailty? Alas! Humanity is feeble, heaven
knows! Very feeble, and unable to support itself. And nobody
knows how circumstances may happen together—to my
thinking, now I could resist the strongest temptation—but
yet I know, 'tis impossible for me to know whether I could or
not, there's no certainty in things of this life. Oh, Lord, ask
me the question! I'll swear I'll refuse it: I swear I'll deny it—
therefore, don't ask me, nay you shan't ask me, I swear I'll
deny it. Oh Gemini, you have brought all the blood into my
face; I warrant I am as red as a turkey cock. Oh, fie, Cousin
Mellefont! Hear you? No, no; I'll deny you first, and hear you

afterwards: For one does not know how one's mind may change upon hearing—hearing is one of the senses, and all the senses are fallible; I won't trust my honor, I assure you; my honor is fallible and un-come-at-able. Oh, name it no more—bless you, how can you talk of heaven, and have so much wickedness in your heart? Maybe you don't think it a sin—they say some of you gentlemen don't think it a sin— maybe it is no sin to them that don't think it so—indeed, if I did not think it a sin—but still my honor, if it were no sin— but then, to marry my daughter, for the conveniency of frequent opportunities—I'll never consent to that, as sure as can be, I'll break the match. Nay, nay, rise up, come, you shall see my good nature. I know love is powerful, and nobody can help his passion: I know 'tis not your fault nor I swear it is not mine. How can I help it if I have charms? And how can you help it, if you are made a captive? I swear it's a pity it should be a fault,—but my honor—well, but your honor, too—but the sin!—Well, but the necessity—oh, Lord, here's somebody coming, I dare not stay. Well, you must consider of your crime, and strive as much as can be against it—strive be sure—but don't be melancholy, don't despair—but never think that I'll grant you anything; oh, Lord, no;—but be sure you lay aside all thoughts of marriage, for though I know you don't love Cynthia, only as a blind for your passion to me; yet it will make me jealous—oh, Lord, what did I say? Jealous? No, no, I can't be jealous, for I must not love you—therefore, don't hope—but don't despair neither,—oh, they're coming, I must fly!

The Distress'd Wife

John Gay   *Act II, scene v, vi; Comic*

Lady Willit: If Mr. Forward calls, I think—Yes—you *may* let
him in. Not no one living Creature besides. [Going] Hold—
Where is the stupid fellow going? [Returns] And Lord
Courtlove, too.—No—Tis no matter. But be sure you let me
know when he is with Miss Sprightly. The Fellow cannot be
such a blockhead as to deny me to him—You know he is
always admitted. Have I not sent to Lady Frankair twice this
morning? If she is not here in five minutes, order the foot-
man to go again.—Now you know my commands. But be
sure you let in no Fusties.

How happy is that creature! Of all the women in the
world, I envy Lady Frankair. She hath her will in every thing,
be it ever so unreasonable. Then too, she hath not (like most
of our fine Ladies) lost her reputation, I should say gain'd a
reputation, for nothing. Besides, who could live more ele-
gantly? Who dresses better? Who hath more command in her
family? Who plays deeper or handsomer? Who hath the credit of more intrigues, and hath really had 'em? Half of the
women in town have had nothing but the Vanity of having
lost their reputation. Sure there was a time, when men and
women had other pleasures besides Vanity. The flirting fel-
lows now play at making love, as the children make believe
gossip and christenings. But, Lady Frankair; sure, she hath
more wit and more real pleasure! Would I were that very
individual woman! And wouldst thou really, Fetch, have a
women deny herself the use of her husband's fortune? [sits
down] Thou talkest so like my husband, there's no bearing
thee. I have an aversion to any body that is so intolerably
wise. Why dost not thou talk to me too of Economy? I am
surfeited with that hideous word. Don't you know we have
company to dinner, and that I am to be dress'd today? Nay,

prithee, Wench, don't lay violent hands upon me. I won't dress yet. See if the Tea-things are ready.

The Dutch Courtesan

John Marston   *Act III, scene iii; Comic*

Mistress Mulligrub: Nay, I pray you, stay and drink. And how
does your mistress? I know her very well; I have been inward
with her, and so has many more. She was ever a good,
patient, creature, i' faith. With all my heart, I'll remember
your master, an honest man; he knew me before I was married. An honest man he is, and a crafty. He comes forward in
the world well, I warrant him; and his wife is a proper
woman, that she is. Well, she has been as proper a woman as
any in Cheap; she paints now, and yet she keeps her husband's old customers to him still. In troth, a fine-fac'd woman
in a wainscot carved seat is a worthy ornament to a trades-
man's shop, and an attractive, I warrant; her husband shall
find it in the custom of his ware, I'll assure him. God be with
you, good youth. I acknowledge the receipt. I acknowledge
all the receipt—sure, 'tis very well spoken! I acknowledge the
receipt! This 'tis to have good education and to be brought
up in a tavern. I do keep as gallant and as good company,
though I say it, as any she in London. Squires, gentlemen,
and knights diet at my table, and I do lend some of them
money; and full many fine men go upon my score, as simple
as I stand here, and I trust them; and truly, they very knightly
and courtly promise fair, give me very good words, and a
piece of flesh when time of year serves. Nay, though my husband be a citizen and's cap's made of wool, yet I ha' wit and
can see my good as soon as another; for I have all the thanks.
My silly husband, alas, he knows nothing of it; 'tis I that
bear—'tis I that must bear a brain for all.

The Dutch Courtesan

John Marston   *Act III, scene i; Comic*

Crispinella: Pish, sister Beatrice! prithee read no more; my
stomach o' late stands against kissing extremely . . . By the
faith and trust I bear to my face, 'tis grown one of the most
unsavory ceremonies. Body o' beauty, 'tis one of the most
unpleasing, injurious customs to ladies. Any fellow that has
but one nose on his face, and standing collar and skirts also
lined with taffety silk, must salute us on the lips as familiar-
ly—Soft skins save us! there was a stub bearded John-a Stile
with a ployden's face saluted me last day and stuck his bristle
through my lips; I ha' spent ten shillings in pomatum since to
skin them again. Marry, if a nobleman or a knight with one
lock visit us, though his unclean goose-turd-green teeth ha'
the palsy, his nostrils smell worse than a putrified maribone,
and his loose beard drops into our bosom, yet we must kiss
him with a curtsy. A curse! for my part, I had as lief they
would break wind in my lips. Let's ne'er be ashamed to speak
what we be not ashamed to think; I dare as boldly speak venery as think venery. Now bashfulness seize you! we pronounce
boldly robbery, murder, treason, which deeds must needs be
far more loathsome than an act which is so natural, just, and
necessary as that of procreation. You shall have an hypocriti-
cal vestal virgin speak that with close teeth publicly. For my
own part, I consider nature without apparel, without disguis-
ing of custom or compliment. I give thoughts words, and
words truth, and truth boldness. She whose honest freeness
makes it her virtue to speak what she thinks will make it her
necessity to think what is good. I love no prohibited things,
and yet I would have nothing prohibited by policy but by
virtue; for, as in the fashion of time, those books that are
called in are most in sale and request, so in nature those
actions that are most prohibited are most desired. . . . Fie, fie!

Virtue is a free, pleasant, buxom quality. I love a constant countenance well; but this froward, ignorant coyness, sour, austere, lumpish, uncivil privateness, that promises nothing but rough skins and hard stools, ha! Fie on't! Good for nothing but nothing.

The Dutch Courtesan

John Marston   *Act III, scene i; Comic*

Crispinella: Marry? No, faith; husbands are like lots in the lot-
tery: you may draw forty blanks before you find one that has
any prize in him. A husband generally is a careless, domineer-
ing thing that grows like coral, which as long as it is under
water is soft and tender, but as soon as it has got his branch
above the waves is presently hard, stiff, not to be bowed but
burst; so when your husband is a suitor and under your
choice, Lord, how supple he is, how obsequious, how at your
service, sweet lady! Once married, got up his head above, a
stiff, crooked, knobby, inflexible, tyrannous creature he
grows; then they turn like water: more you would embrace,
the less you hold. I'll live my own woman, and if the worst
come to the worst, I had rather price a wag than a fool. . . .
Virtuous marriage? There is no more affinity betwixt virtue
and marriage than betwixt a man and his horse. Indeed,
virtue gets up upon marriage sometimes and manageth it in
the right way, but marriage is of another piece; for as a horse
may be without a man, and a man without a horse, so marriage, you know, is often without virtue, and virtue, I am
sure, more oft without marriage. But thy match, sister, by my
troth, I think 'twill do well. He's a well-shaped, clean-lipped
gentleman, of a handsome but not affected fineness, a good
faithful eye, and a well-humored cheek. Would he did not
stoop in the shoulders, for thy sake.

Hyde Park

James Shirley   Act I, scene ii; Comic

Mistress Carol: You do intend to marry him, then?
    What is in your condition makes you weary?
    You are sick of plenty and command; you have
    Too, too much liberty, too many servants;
    Your jewels are your own, and you would see
    How they will show upon your husband's wagtail.
    You have a coach now, and a Christian livery
    To wait on you to church, and are not catechised
    When you come home; you have a waiting woman,
    A monkey, squirrel, and a brace of islands,
    Which may be thought superfluous in your family
    When husbands come to rule. A pretty wardrobe,
    A tailor of your own, a doctor, too,
    That knows your body, and can make you sick
    I' the spring, or fall, or when you have a mind to't,
    Without control. You have the benefit
    Of talking loud and idle at your table,
    May sing a wanton ditty, and not be chid;
    Dance and go late to bed, say your own prayers,
    Or go to Heaven by your chaplain.
    And you will lose all this, for
    "I, Cicely, take thee, John, to be my husband?"
    Keep him still to be your servant;
    Imitate me; a hundred suitors cannot
    Be half the trouble of one husband. I
    Dispose my frowns and favors like a princess;
    Deject, advance, undo, create again;
    It keeps the subjects in obedience,
    And teaches 'em to look at me with distance.

I'll Tell You What

Elizabeth Inchbald   *Act II, scene i; Comic*

Lady Euston: No, no, Sir George, a fond wife will never suffer her husband to revenge her wrongs at so great a risk: Besides, the exertion of a little thought and fancy will more powerfully vindicate innocence, than that brilliant piece of steel, I assure you . . . Now, suppose a gentleman makes love to me—I divulge the affront to you; you call my insulter to account—Your ball misses; he fires into the air; and, to the fame of having dared to wound your honor, he gains that of presenting you with your life. . . . Well, then, we will suppose he kills you; how do you like that? . . . There is as severe a punishment to men of gallantry (as they call themselves) as sword or pistol: laugh at them; that is a ball which cannot miss; and yet kills only their vanity . . . Let me see; we have been now only three months married; and in that short time, I have had no less than five or six men of fashion to turn into ridicule. The first who ventured to declare his passion was Lord William Bloomly; his rank, joined to his uncommon beauty, had insured him success; and wherever I went, I was certain to hear his distress whispered in my ear; and at every opportunity he fell even upon his knees; and, as a tender earnest of my pity for him, begged, with all the eloquence of love, for a single lock of my hair, which he would value more than any other woman's person; the wealth of worlds; or (he is a great patriot, you know), even the welfare of his country. . . . I promised him this single lock . . . and added, with a blush, that I must insist on a few hairs from his eyebrows in return, which he absolutely refused;—and, on my urging it, was obliged to confess, "he valued that little brown arch more than the lock he had been begging for; consequently, more than any woman's person; the wealth of worlds, or even the welfare of his country." I immediately circulated this anecdote and exhibited the gentleman, both as a gallant and a patriot; and now his lordships' eyebrow, which was once the admiration, is become the ridicule of every drawing room. . . . "You are the most beautiful woman I ever saw," said Lord Bandy; "and your lordship is positively the most lovely of mankind."—"What eyes," cried he; "what hair," cried I; "what lips," continued he; "what teeth," added I; "what a hand and arm," said he; "and what a leg and foot," said I;—"Your ladyship is jesting," was his lordship's last reply; and he has never since even paid me one compliment. Prudes censure my conduct; I am too free—while their favorite, Lady Strenuous, in another corner of the ballroom, cries to her admirer—"Desists, my lord, or my dear Sir Charles shall know that you dare thus to wound my ears with your licentious passion; if you ever presume to breathe it again, I will acquaint him with it—Depend upon it I will. [Sighs and languishes] Oh! You have destroyed my peace of mind forever." Now, with your consent, what must be the confusion, shame, and disappointment, of my two masked lovers tomorrow evening; the brutal audacity of one, and insignificance of the other; both beneath your resentment, yet deserving objects of mine. And, indeed, Sir George, it is my fixed opinion that, the man who would endeavor to wrong a virtuous wife, should be held too despicable for the resentment of the husband, and only worth the debasement inflicted by our sex.

Madam Fickle

Thomas Durfey *Act IV, scene ii; Comic*

Fickle: Ha, ha, ha, ha—
  That heaven should give man so proud a heart,
  And yet so little knowledge—Silly creature,
  That talks, and laughs, and kisses oft that hand
  That steals away its reason as if nature
  Had played the traitor and seduced the sex,
  Without the aid of destiny, or women.
  Ah, with what pleasant ease
  The bird may be ensnared—Set but a wanton look,
  You catch whole coveys; nay there is magic
  Pertaining to our sex, that draws 'em in,
  Though in the long vacation—and by heaven,
  I am resolved to work my sly deceits
  Till my revenge is perfect—Thus far I've done well,
  And I'll persevere in the mystery,
  Wheedle 'em to the snare with cunning plots;
  Then bring it off with quick designing wit,
  And quirks of dubious meaning. Turn and wind
  Like fox, in a storm, to prey on all,
  And yet be thought a saint—Thus queen I'll sit,
  And hell shall laugh to see a woman's wit.

The Man of Mode

George Etherege   *Act V, scene i; Comic*

Mrs. Loveit: Is there a thing so hateful as a senseless mimic? A ridiculous animal, who has more of the ape than the ape has of the man in him. Those noisy fools, however you despise 'em, have good qualities, which weigh more—or ought at least—with us women than all the pernicious wit you have to boast of. First, they really admire us, while you at best but flatter us well. There is no fear they should deceive us. Then, they are assiduous, sir, they are ever offering us their service, and always waiting on our will. Their conversation, too, diverts us better. Were it sillier than you can make it, you must allow 'tis pleasanter to laugh at others than to be laughed at ourselves, though never so wittily. Then, though they want skill to flatter us, they flatter themselves so well, they save us the labor. We need not take that care and pains to satisfy 'em of our love which we so often lose on you. They have an implicit faith in us which keeps 'em from prying narrowly into our secrets, and saves us the vexatious trouble of clearing doubts which your subtle and causeless jealousies every moment raise. The man who loves above his quality does not suffer more than the insolent impertinence of his mistress than the woman who loves above her understanding does from the arrogant presumptions of her friend. The old and the ill favored are only fit for properties, indeed, but young and handsome fools have met with kinder fortunes. Had I not with a dear experience bought the knowledge of your falsehood, you might have fooled me yet. This is not the first jealousy you have feigned to make a quarrel with me, and get a week to throw away on some such unknown inconsiderable slut as you have been lately lurking with at plays. You take a pride of late in using of me ill, that the town may know the power you have over me; which now—as unreasonably as yourself—expects that I—do me all the injuries you can—must love you still. What made you come to disturb my growing quiet? Insupportable! Insulting devil! This from you, the only author of my shame! This from another had been but justice, but from you 'tis a hellish and inhuman outrage. What have I done? I walked last night with Sir Fopling. You, who have more pleasure in the ruin of a woman's reputation than in the endearments of her love, reproach me not with yourself, and I defy you to name the man can lay a blemish on my fame. Stay—I hate that nauseous fool, you know I do. Y'had raised my anger equal to my love, a thing you ne'er could do before, and in revenge I did—I know not what I did. Would you would not think on't any more. 'Twill be believed a jealous spite. Come, forget it.

The Obstinate Lady

Sir Aston Cokain   *Act I, scene iii; Comic*

Antiphila [reading]:
> "Fair Antiphila hath hair
> Would grace the Paphian queen to wear;
> Fit to tune heaven's lute withal,
> When the gods for music call;
> Fit to make a veil to hide
> Aurora's blushes each morning tide;
> Fit to compose a crafty gin
> To take the hearts of lookers in;
> Able to make the stubborn kind,
> And, who dislike it, t'be judged blind.
> Though it is soft and fine it ties
> My heart that it in fetters lies."

It is a neat—I know not what. I have not poetry enough in me to give it a name. These lovers are the prettiest fools, I think, in the world; and 'twere not for them, I cannot tell what we women should do. We desire nothing more than to be praised, and their love to us will do it beyond our wishes. I gave Phylander, upon his long importunity, a lock of hair and see into what a vein it has put him! I'm sorry he had it not a week sooner; I should then, perhaps, ha'had a sonnet-book ere this. 'Tis pity wit should lie obscurely within any, that a lock will give it vent. I love him not; I should rather choose his father, who is as earnest a suitor to me as he. Yet I know, because of his age, very few ladies would be of my mind; but as yet, I care for neither of them.

Polly Honeycombe

George Colman   *Scene 1; Comic*

Polly: [With a book in her hand] Well said, Sir George!—O the
dear man!—But so—[Reading] 'With these words the enraptured baronet concluded his declaration of love.'

   This is a most beautiful passage, I protest! Well, a novel for
my money. Oh, Nurse, I am glad to see you—Well, and
how—tell me, tell me all this instant. Did you see him? Did
you give him my letter? Did he write? Will he come? Shall I
see him? Have you got the letter in your pocket? Come, give
me the letter, the answer to mine. Come then! Pshah! Send it
some time today? I wonder now, [musing] how he will convey it. Will he squeeze it, as he did the last, into the chicken-
house in the garden? Or will he write it in lemon juice, and
send it in a book, like blank paper? Or will he throw it into
the house, enclosed in an orange? I have not read so many
books for nothing. Novels, Nursee, novels! A novel is the only
thing to teach a girl life, and the way of the world, and ele-
gant fancies, and love to the end of the chapter . . . [Looking
into the book] 'She raved, but the baronet'—I really think I
love Mr. Scribble as well as Emilia did Sir George.—Do you
think, Nursee, I should have had such a good notion of love
so early, if I had not read novels?—Did I not make a conquest of Mr. Scribble in a single night at dancing? But my
cross papa will hardly ever let me go out.—And then I know
life as well as if I had been in the beau monde all my days. I
can tell the nature of a masquerade as well as I had been at
twenty. I long for a mobbing-scene with Mr. Scribble to the
two-shilling gallery, or a snug party a little way out of town,
in a post-chaise—and then I have such a head full of
intrigues and contrivances! Oh, Nursee a novel is the only
thing! I tell you what, Nursee. I'll marry Mr. Scribble, and
not marry Mr. Ledger, whether papa and mama choose it or

no. And how do you think I'll contrive it? Why, don't you know? O, lord, it's the commonest thing in the world—I intend to elope! Yes, run away, to be sure. Why, there's nothing in that, you know. Every girl elopes, when her parents are obstinate and ill-natured about marrying her. It was just so with Betsy Thompson, and Sally Wilkins, and Clarinda, and Leonora in the History of Dick Careless, and Julia, in the Adventures of Tom Ramble, and fifty others—did not they all elope? And so will I, too. I have as much right to elope as they had, for I have as much love and as much spirit as the best of them. What care I for papa and mama? Have they not been married and happy long enough ago? And are they not still coaxing and fondling, and kissing each other all the day long? [Mimicking] "Where's my dear love, my beauty?" says papa, hobbling along with his crutch-headed cane, and his old gouty legs. "Ah, my sweeting, my precious Mr. Honeycombe, d'ye love your own dear wife?" says mama; and then they squeeze their hard hands to each other, and their old eyes twinkle, and they're as loving as Darby and Joan—especially if mama has had a cordial or two—eh, Nursee! And then, perhaps, in comes my utter aversion, Mr. Ledger, with his news from the Change, and his Change-alley wit, and his thirty percent and [Mimicking] stocks have risen one and a half and three eighths. I'll tell ye what, Nursee! They would make fine characters for a novel, all three of them.

The Provoked Wife

Sir John Vanbrugh   Act I, scene i; Comic

Lady Brute: The devil's in the fellow, I think. I was told before I
married him that thus 'twould be. But I thought I had
charms enough to govern him; and that where there was an
estate a woman must needs be happy; so my vanity has
deceived me and my ambition has made me uneasy. But
some comfort still: if one would be revenged of him, these are
good times. A woman may have a gallant and a separate
maintenance, too. The surly puppy! Yet he's a fool for't. For
hitherto he has been no monster, but who knows how far he
may provoke me. I never loved him, yet I have been ever true
to him, and that in spite of all the attacks of art and nature
upon poor weak woman's heart in favor of a tempting lover.
Methinks so noble a defense as I have made should be
rewarded with a better usage. Or who can tell? Perhaps a
good part of what I suffer from my husband may be a judgment upon me for my cruelty to my lover. Lord, with what
pleasure could I indulge that thought, were there but a possi-
bility of finding arguments to make it good. And how do I
know but there may? Let me see. What opposes? My matri-
monial vow? Why, what did I vow? I think I promised to be
true to my husband. Well, and he promised to be kind to me.
But he hasn't kept his word. Why then, I'm absolved from
mine. Aye, that seems clear to me. The argument's good
between the king and the people, why not between the husband and the wife? O, but that condition was not expressed.
No matter, 'twas understood. Well, by all I see, if I argue the
matter a little longer with myself, I shan't find so many bug-
bears in the way as I thought I should. Lord, what fine
notions of virtue do we women take up upon the credit of
old foolish philosophers. Virtue's its own reward, virtue's this,
virtue's that. Virtue's an ass, and a gallant's worth forty on't.

The Rivals

Richard Brinsley Sheridan   *Act I, scene ii; Comic*

Lydia: Ah, Julia, I have a thousand things to tell you! Before we
are interrupted, let me impart to you some of my distress; I
know your gentle nature will sympathize with me, though
your prudence may condemn me. My letters have informed
you of my whole connection with Beverley, but I have lost
him, my Julia—my aunt has discovered our intercourse, by a
note she intercepted, and has confined me since. Yet would
you believe it? She has fallen absolutely in love with a tall
Irish baronet she met one night since we have been here, at
Lady MacShuffle's rout. She really carries on a kind of corre-
spondence with him, under a feigned name, though, till she
chooses to be known to him; but it is a Delia, or a Celia, I
assure you. Since she has discovered her own frailty, she has
become ten times more suspicious of mine. Therefore I must
inform you of another plague; that odious Acres is to be in
Bath today, so that, I protest, I shall be teased out of all spirits. But you have not heard the worst. Unfortunately I had
quarreled with my poor Beverley, just before my aunt made
the discovery, and I have not seen him since to make up. I
don't know how it was, as often as we had been together, we
had never had a quarrel; and, somehow, I was afraid he would
never give me an opportunity. So, last Thursday, I wrote a
letter to myself, to inform myself that Beverley was,at that
time, paying his addresses to another woman. I signed it
"Your unknown friend," showed it to Beverley, charged him
with falsehood, put myself in a violent passion, and vowed I'd
never see him more. 'Twas the next day my aunt found the
matter out; I intended only to have teased him three days and
a half, and now I have lost him forever.

The Rivals

Richard Brinsley Sheridan   *Act I, scene ii; Comic*

Mrs. Malaprop: Observe me, Sir Anthony—I would by no means wish a daughter of mine to be a progeny of learning. I don't think so much learning becomes a young woman. For instance—I would never let her meddle with Greek or Hebrew, or Algebra or Simony, or Fluxions, or Paradoxes, or such inflammatory branches of learning; nor will it be necessary for her to handle any of your mathematical, astronomical, diabolical instruments; but, Sir Anthony, I would send her, at nine years old, to a boarding school, in order to learn a little ingenuity and artifice. Then sir, she should have a supercilious knowledge in accounts; and, as she grew up, I would have her instructed in geometry, that she might know something of the contagious countries. Above all, she should not mispronounce or misspell words as our young ladies of the present day constantly do. This, Sir Anthony, is what I would have a woman know; and I don't think there is a superstitious article in it.

The Rivals

Richard Brinsley Sheridan   *Act V, scene i; Comic*

Lydia: Oh, Julia, I am come to you with such an appetite for consolation! Lud, child! What's the matter with you? You have been crying! I'll be hanged if that Faulkland has not been tormenting you! Whatever vexations you may have, I can assure you mine surpass them. You know who Beverley proves to be? So, then, I see I have been deceived by every one! But I don't care, I'll never have him. Why, is it not the provoking, when I thought we were coming to the prettiest distress imaginable, to find myself made a mere Smithfield bargain of at last? There had I projected one of the most sentimental elopements! So becoming a disguise—so amiable a ladder of ropes—conscious moon—four horses—Scotch parson—with such surprise to Mrs. Malaprop, and such paragraphs in the newspapers! Oh, I shall die with disappointment! Now, sad reverse! What have I to expect but after a deal of flimsy preparation, with a bishop's license and my aunt's blessing, to go simpering up to the altar, or, perhaps, be cried three time in a country church, and have an unmannerly fat clerk as the consent of every butcher in the parish, to join John Absolute and Lydia Languish, spinster. Oh, that I should live to hear myself called spinster! How mortifying to remember the dear, delicious shifts I used to be put to to gain half a minute's conversation with this fellow! How often have I stole forth in the coldest night in January, and found him in the garden, stuck like a dripping statue! There would he kneel to me in the snow, and sneeze and cough so pathetically—shivering with cold, and I with apprehension—and, while the freezing blast numbed our joints, how warmly would he press me to pity his flame and glow with mutual ardor! Ah, Julia, that was something like being in love!

The Rover

Aphra Behn   *scene ix; Comic*

Hellena: You see, captain, how willing I am to be friends with you, til time and ill luck make us lovers; and ask you the question first rather than put your modesty to the blush by asking me. For, alas, I know you captains are such strict men, and such severe observers of your vows to chastity, that 'twill be hard to prevail with your tender conscience to marry a young willing maid. O' my conscience, that will be our destiny because we are both of one humor. I am as inconstant as you. For I have considered, captain, that a handsome woman has a great deal to do whilst her face is good, for then is our harvest-time to gather friends. And should I in these days of my youth catch a fit or foolish constancy, I were undone; 'tis loitering by daylight in our great journey. Therefore, I declare I'll allow by one year for love, one year for indifference, and one year for hate, and then go hang yourself, for I profess myself the gay, the kind, and the inconstant. The devil's in't if this won't please you!

Three Weeks After Marriage

Samuel Foote   *Act I; Comic*

Lady Racket: [Coming on] Oh la! I am quite fatigued. I can
hardly move. Why don't you help me, you barbarous man?
. . . Dear me, this glove! Why don't you help me off with my
glove? Pshaw! You awkward thing, let it alone! You aren't fit
to be about my person. I might as well not be married, for
any use you are of. Reach me a chair. You have no compassion for me. I am so glad to sit down! Why do you drag me
to routs? You know I hate them. I'm out of humor. I lost all
my money. I hate gaming. It almost metamorphoses a
woman into a fury. Do you know that I was frighted at
myself several times tonight? I had a huge oath at the very tip
of my tongue. . . . I caught myself at it, but I bit my lips and
so I did not disgrace myself. And then I was crammed up in a
corner of the room with such a strange party at a whist table,
looking at black and red spots. Did you mind them? There
was that strange, unaccountable woman, Mrs. Nightshade.
She behaved so strangely to her husband, a poor, inoffensive,
good natured, good sort of a good for nothing kind of man,
but she so teased him—'How could you play that card? Ah,
you have a head and so has a pin! You are a numskull, you
know you are—Madam, he has the poorest head in the
world, he does not know what he is about—you know you
don't—Ah, fie! I am ashamed of you." And then, to crown
all, there was my Lady Clackit, who runs on with an eternal
larum of nothing, out of all season, time and place. In the
very midst of the game, she begins, "Lard, m'em, I was appre-
hensive I should not be able to wait on your ladyship—my
poor little dog Pompey—the sweetest thing in the world—a
spade led!—there's the knave—I was fetching a walk, m'em,
the other morning in the Park; a fine, frosty morning it was; I
love frosty weather of all things. Let me look at the last

trick—and so, m'em, little Pompey—Oh! if your la'yship was to see the dear little creature pinched with the frost, and mincing his steps along the Mall, with his pretty little innocent face—I vow I don't know what to play—and so, m'em, while I was talking to Captain Flimsey—Your la'yship knows Captain Flimsey?—Nothing but rubbish in my hand—I can't help it—and so, m'em, five odious frights of dogs beset my poor little Pompey—the dear creature has the heart of a lion, but who can resist five at once? And so Pompey barked for assistance. The hurt he received was upon his chest. The doctor would not advise him to venture out till the wound was healed for fear of an inflammation—Pray, what's trumps?" Why don't you hand me upstairs? Oh, I am so tired. Let us go to rest.

The Way To Keep Him

Arthur Murphy   *Act I, scene ii; Comic*

Muslin: Dear Ma'am, why will you chagrin yourself about a vile man, that is not worth, no, as I live and breathe, not worth a single sigh? If I was you, I'd do for him; as I'm a living Christian, I would.—If I could not cure my grief, I'd find some comforts, that's what I would do. No comfort, Ma'am? Whose fault then? Would anybody but you, Ma'am? It provokes me to think of it. Would anybody, Ma'am, as young and handsome as you are, with so many accomplishments, Ma'am, sit at home, as melancholy as a poor servant out of place? And all this for what? Why, for a husband, and such a husband! What do you think the world will say of you, Ma'am, if you go on this way? . . . Lard, Ma'am, to be forever pining and grieving! Dear heart! If all the women in London, in your case, were to sit down and die of the spleen, what would become of all the public places? They might turn Vauxhall to a hop-garden, make a brewhouse of Ranelagh, and let both the playhouses to a Methodist preacher. We should not have the racketting with 'em we have now.— "John, let the horses be put to."—"John, go to my Lady Trumpabout's and invite her to a small party of twenty or thirty card tables."—"John, run to My Lady Cat Gut, and let her Ladyship know I'll wait on her to the new opera."— "John, run as fast as ever you can, with my compliments to Mr. Varney, and tell him I shall take it as the greatest favor on earth if he will let me have a side box for the new play—No excuses, tell him."—They whisk about the town, and rantipole it with as unconcerned looks, and as florid outsides as if they were treated at home like so many goddesses, though everybody knows possession has ungoddessed them all long ago, and their husbands care no more for them—no, by jingo, no more than they do for their husbands. Dear

Ma'am, tis enough to make a body run on.—If everybody thought like you.

[Ending #1]

. . . A brass thimble for love, if it is not answered by love.— What the deuce is here to do? Shall I go and fix my heart upon a man, that shall despise me for that very reason, and, "Ay," says he, "poor fool, I see she loves me—the woman's well enough, only she has one inconvenient circumstance about her: I'm married to her, and marriage is the Devil."— And then when he's going a-roguing, smiles impudently in your face, and, "My dear, divert yourself, I'm just going to kill half an hour at the chocolate-house, or to peep in at the play; your servant, my dear, your servant."—Fie upon 'em! I know 'em all.—Give me a husband that will enlarge the circle of my innocent pleasures: but a husband nowadays, Ma'am, is no such a thing.—A husband now, as I hope for mercy, is nothing at all but a scarecrow, to show you the fruit, but touch it if you dare.—A husband—The Devil take 'em all— Lord forgive one for swearing—is nothing at all but a bug- bear, a snapdragon; a husband, Ma'am is a mere monster; that is to say, if one makes him so; then, for certain, he is a monster indeed; and if one does not make him so, then he behaves like a monster, and of the two evils, by my troth— Ma'am, was you ever at the play of Catherine and Mercutio? The vile man calls his wife his goods, and his cattles, and his household stuff.—There you may see, Ma'am, what a hus- band is—a husband is—but here comes one will tell you— Here comes Sir Brilliant Fashion—Ask his advice, Ma'am. I protest and vow, Ma'am, I think Sir Brilliant a very pretty gentlemen. He's the very pink of fashion; he dresses fashion- ably, lives fashionably, wins your money fashionably, loses his own fashionably, and does everything fashionably; and then, he is so lively, and talks so lively, and so much to say, and so never at a loss.—But here he comes.

[Ending #2]

97

The Way To Keep Him

Arthur Murphy   *Act II, scene i; Comic*

Mrs. Bellmour: Repairs her smiles, my lord! I don't like the application of that phrase.—Pray, my lord, are my smiles out of repair, like an old house in the country, that wants a tenant? And so you think I really want a tenant? And perhaps you can imagine too that I am going to put up a bill to signify to all passers-by that here is a mansion to let. Well, I swear, I don't think it would be a bad scheme. I have a great mind to do so. But I'll let it to none but a single gentleman, that you may depend upon. And then it must be a lease for life—but nobody will be troubled with it—I shall never get it off my hands. Do you think I shall, my lord? . . . Heavens, what a dying swain you are! And does your Lordship really intend to be guilty of matrimony? Lord, what a question have I asked? Well, to be sure, I am a very madcap! My lord, don't you think me a strange madcap? I hate your pensive, melancholy beauty, that sits like a well grown vegetable in a room for an hour together, till at last she is animated to the violent exertion of saying yes or no, and then enters into a matter of fact conversation: "Have you heard the news? Miss Beverly is going to be married to Captain Shoulderknot.—My Lord Mortgage has had another tumble at Arthur's; Sir William Squanderstock has lost his election. They say short aprons are coming into fashion again." Pray, my lord, have you ever observed the manner of one lady's accosting another at Ranelagh? She comes up to you with a demure look of insipid serenity—makes you a solemn salute—"Ma'am, I am overjoyed to meet you—you look charmingly.—But, dear Madam, did you hear what happened to us all the other night? We were going home from the opera, Ma'am; you know my Aunt Roly-Poly—it was her coach—there was she, and Lady Betty Fidget—your most obedient servant, Ma'am

—Lady Betty, you know, is recovered—everybody thought it over with her, but Dr. Snakeroot was called in, no not Dr. Snakeroot, Dr. Bolus it was, and so he altered the course of the medicines, and so my Lady Betty recovered; well, there was she and Sir George Bragwell—a pretty man Sir George, finest teeth in the world.—Your Ladyship's most obedient.— We expected you last night, but you did not come. He! He!—And so there was he and the rest of us—and so turning the corner of Bond Street, the villain of a coachman over-turned us all; my Aunt Roly-Poly was frightened out of her wits, and Lady Betty has been nervish ever since: only think of that—such accidents in life.—Ma'am, your most obedi-ent—I am proud to see you look so well. And then from this conversation they all run to cards. But one must play some-times—we must let our friends pick our pockets sometimes, or they'll drop our acquaintance.

The Way of the World

William Congreve   *Act IV, scene i; Comic*

Millament: Ah! Idle Creature, get up when you will—and d'ye
hear, I won't be call'd names after I'm married; positively I
won't be call'd names . . . Ay, as wife, spouse, my dear, joy,
jewel, love, sweetheart, and the rest of that nauseous cant, in
which men and their wives are so fulsomely familiar,—- I
shall never bear that,—Good Mirabell, don't let us be familiar
or fond, nor kiss before folks, like my Lady Fadler and Sir
Francis; nor go to Hyde Park together the first Sunday in a
new chariot, to provoke eyes and whispers; And then never to
be seen there together again; as if we were proud of one
another the first week and asham'd of one another for ever
after. Let us never visit together, nor go to a play together,
But let us be very strange and well bred: let us be as strange as
if we had been married a great while; and as well bred as if we
were not marri'd at all . . . Liberty to pay and receive visits to
and from whom I please, to write and receive Letters, without
interrogatories or wry faces on your part. To wear what I
please; and choose conversations only to my own taste; to
have no obligation upon me to converse with wits that I don't
like, because they are your acquaintance; or to be intimate
with fools, because they may be your relations. Come to dinner when I please, dine in my dressing room when I'm out of
humor without giving a reason. To have my closet inviolate;
to be sole-empress of my tea-table, which you must never
presume to approach without first asking leave. And lastly,
where ever I am, you shall always knock at the door before
you come in. These Articles subscrib'd, If I continue to
endure you a little longer, I may by degrees dwindle into a
Wife.

Serio-Comic

The Conscious Lovers

Richard Steele   *Act II, scene ii; Serio-Comic*

Indiana: Well, be not so eager. If he is an ill man, let us look
into his stratagems. Here is another of them. [Showing a let-
ter] Here's two hundred and fifty pounds in bank notes with
these words, "To pay for the set of dressing plate, which will
be brought home tomorrow." Why, dear aunt, now here's
another piece of skill for you which I own I cannot compre-
hend; and it is with a bleeding heart I hear you say anything
to the disadvantage of Mr. Bevil. When he is present, I look
upon him as one to whom I owe my life and the support of
it, then again, as the man who loves me with sincerity and
honor. When his eyes are cast another way and I dare survey
him, my heart is painfully divided between shame and love
. . . This is my state of mind in his presence; and when he is
absent, you are ever dinning my ears with notions of the arts
of men; that his hidden bounty, his respectful conduct, his
careful provision for me after his preserving me from utmost
misery are certain signs he means nothing but to make I
know not what of me. I have, when I am with him, ten thousand things besides my sex's natural decency and shame to
suppress my heart that yearns to thank, to praise, to say it
loves him. I say, thus it is with me while I see him; and in his
absence I am entertained with nothing but your endeavors to
tear this amiable image from my heart and, in its stead, to
place a base dissembler, an artful invader of my happiness,
my innocence, my honor. Go on then, since nothing can
answer you; say what you will of him.

The Constant Couple

George Farquhar   *Act I, scene ii; Serio-Comic*

Lady Lurewell: Parly, my pocket-book! Let me see—Madrid, Venice, Paris, London.—Ay, London! They may talk what they will of the hot countries, but I find love most fruitful under this climate. In a month's space, I have gained—let me see—imprimis, Colonel Standard: as all soldiers should be managed, he shall serve me till I gain my ends, then I disband him. I hate all that don't love me, and slight all that do. Would his whole deluding sex admire me, thus would I slight them all! My virgin and unwary innocence was wronged by faithless man, but now, glance eyes, plot brain, dissemble face, lie tongue, and be a second Eve to tempt, seduce, and damn the lecherous kind. Let me survey my captives.—The Colonel leads out the van; next Mr. Vizard, he courts me, out of the Practice of Piety, therefore is a hypocrite; then Clincher, he adores me with orangery, and is consequently a fool; then my old merchant, Alderman Smuggler, he's a compound of both; out of which medley of lovers, if I don't make good diversion—what d'ye think, Parly? You're a fool, child; observe this, that though a woman swear, forswear, lie, dissemble, back-bite, be proud, vain, malicious, anything, if she secures the main chance, she's still virtuous; that's a maxim. Of all lovers I ever had, Sir Harry was my greatest plague, for I could never make him uneasy. I left him involved in a duel upon my account; I long to know whether the fop be killed or not.

The Contrast

Royall Tyler   *Act I, scene ii; Serio-Comic*

Maria: There is something in this song which ever calls forth my affections. The manly virtue of courage, that fortitude which steels the heart against the keenest misfortunes, which interweaves the laurel of glory amidst the instruments of torture and death, displays something so noble, so exalted, that in despite of the prejudices of education I cannot but admire it, even in a savage. The prepossession which our sex is supposed to entertain for the character of a soldier is, I know, a standing piece of raillery among the wits. A cockade, a lapell'd coat, and a feather, they will tell you, are irresistible by a female heart. Let it be so. Who is it that considers the helpless situation of our sex, that does not see that we each moment stand in need of a protector, and that a brave one, too? Formed of the more delicate materials of nature, endowed only with the softer passions, incapable, from our ignorance of the world, to guard against the wiles of mankind, our security for happiness often depends upon their generosity and courage. Alas, how little of the former do we find! How inconsistent! that man should be leagued to destroy that honor upon which solely rests his respect and esteem. Ten thousand temptations allure us, ten thousand passions betray us; yet the smallest deviation from the path of rectitude is followed by the contempt and insult of man, and the more remorseless pity of woman; years of penitence and tears cannot wash away the stain, nor a life of virtue obliterate its remembrance. Reputation is the life of a woman; yet courage to protect it is masculine and disgusting; and the only safe asylum a woman of delicacy can find is in the arms of a man of honor. How naturally, then, should we love the brave and generous; how gratefully should we bless the arm raised for our protection, when nerv'd by virtue and directed by honor! Heaven grant that the man with whom I may be connected—may be connected! Whither has my imagination transported me—whither does it now lead me? Am I not indissolubly engaged, "by every obligation of honor which by my own consent and my father's approbation can give," to a man who can never share my affections, and whom a few days hence it will be criminal for me to disapprove—to disapprove! Would to heaven that were all—to despise. For, can the most frivolous manners, actuated by the most depraved heart, meet, or merit, anything but contempt from every woman of delicacy and sentiment?

Cutter of Coleman Street

Abraham Cowley   *Act II, scene i; Serio-Comic*

Aurelia: I see 'tis no small part of policy
To keep some small spies in an enemy's quarters:
The Parliament had reason—
I would not for five hundred pounds but ha' corrupted my
cousin Lucia's maid; and yet it costs me nothing but Sack-
possets, and Wine, and Sugar when her mistress is a-bed, and
tawdry ribbonds, or fine trimm'd gloves sometimes, and once
I think a pair of counterfeit ruby pendants that cost me half a
crown. The poor wench loves dy'd glass like any Indian; for a
diamond bob I'd have her Maidenhead, if I were a Man, and
she a Maid. If her mistress did but talk in her sleep sometimes, o' my conscience, she'd sit up all night and watch her,
only to tell me in the morning what she said; 'Tis the prettiest diligent wretch in her calling, now she has undertaken't.
Her intelligence just now was very good and
May be o' consequence; That young Truman is
Stoln up the back way into my Cousin's chamber.
These are your grave Maids that study Romances, and will be
All Madonnas and Cassandras, and never spit but by the
Rules of Honor; Oh, here she comes, I hope, with fresh intel-
ligence from the foe's rendezvous.

Fatal Curiosity

George Lillo   Act I, scene ii; Serio-Comic

Charlot: What's this? A letter superscribed to me!
   None could covey it here but you, Maria.
   Ungen'rous, cruel maid! To use me thus,
   To join with flatt'ring men to break my peace,
   And persecute me to the last retreat!
   No matter whence, return it back unopened!
   I have no love, no charms but for my Wilmot,
   Nor would have any. I'll not despair
   (Patience shall cherish hope), nor wrong his honor
   By unjust suspicion. I know his truth,
   And will preserve my own. But to prevent
   All future vain, officious importunity,
   Know, thou incessant foe to my repose,
   Whether he sleeps secure from mortal care
   In the deep bosom of the bois'trous main,
   Or, tossed, with tempests, still endures its rage;
   Whether his weary pilgrimage by land
   Has found an end and he now rests in peace
   In earth's cold womb, or wanders o'er her face;
   Be it my lot to waste, in pining grief,
   The remnants of my days for his known loss
   Or live, as now, uncertain and in doubt,
   No second choice shall violate my vows.
   High Heaven, which heard them and abhors the perjured,
   Can witness they were made without reserve,
   Never to be retracted, ne'er dissolved
   By accidents or absence, time or death!

Fatal Curiosity

George Lillo   *Act III, scene i; Serio-Comic*

Agnes: Who should this stranger be? And then this casket—
   He says it is of value, and yet trusts it,
   As if a trifle, to a stranger's hand.
   His confidence amazes me. Perhaps
   It is not what he says. I'm strongly tempted
   To open it and see. No, let it rest.
   Why should my curiosity excite me
   To search and pry into th'affairs of others,
   Who have t'employ my thoughts so many cares
   And sorrows of my own? With how much ease
   The spring gives way! Surprising! Most prodigious!
   My eyes are dazzled and my ravished heart
   Leaps at the glorious sight. How bright's the lustre,
   How immense the worth of these fair jewels!
   Aye, such a treasure would expel forever
   Base poverty and all its abject train:
   The mean devices we're reduced to use
   To keep famine and preserve our lives
   From day to day, the cold neglect of friends,
   The galling scorn or more provoking pity
   Of an insulting world. Possessed of these,
   Plenty, content, and power might take their turn,
   And lofty pride bare its aspiring head
   At our approach and once more bend before us.
   A pleasing dream!—'Tis past, and now I wake
   More wretched by the happiness I've lost.
   For sure it was a happiness to think
   Though but a moment, such a treasure mine.
   Nay it was more than thought. I saw and touched
   The bright temptation, and I see it yet.
   'Tis here—'tis mine—I have it in possession!

Must I resign it? Must I give it back?
Am I in love with misery and want,
To rob myself and court so vast a loss?
Retain it, then! But how? There is a way—
Why sinks my heart? Why does my blood run cold?
Why am I thrilled with horror? 'Tis not choice,
But dire necessity, suggests the thought!

Love Tricks

James Shirley   *Act III, scene ii; Serio-Comic*

Selina [in shepherd's weeds]: Thus far have I passed without dis-
covery: the morning is auspicious to my flight. Selina, what
an alteration hath a day made in thee, that, to prevent thy so
desired marriage, thou art thus lost in a masculine habit, and
dost fly him, thou didst so much love, aged Rufaldo! In what
a lethargy wert thou fallen, Selina!
Whither had reason so withdrawn itself,
I could not make distinction of a man,
From such a heap of age, aches, and rheum?
Sure I was mad; and it doth increase my fury
To think with what a violence I ran
To embrace such rottenness. Oh, my guilty soul
Doth feel the punishment of the injury
I did to Infortunio of late;
Of whom as I despair, so shall the world,
Ever to know again hapless Selina.
This is the morn the sacred rites should tie
Me to Rufaldo, ripe in expectation;
But, like Ixion, he shall grasp a cloud,
My empty clothes at home: Selina thus
Is turn's a shepherd, and will try her fortune:
Hard by the shepherds have their shady dwellings,
There let Selina end her hapless days.
Father and all farewell! Thus, as Felice,
My other sister, I'll wear out my life,
Far from your knowledge: sacred Love commands
Revenge and justice for my cruelty,
And reason, now awak'd, shall lead me to it.
Thus I am safe; I go to find out that
Will meet me everywhere—a just sad fate.

The Maid's Revenge

James Shirley   *Act II, scene iii; Serio-Comic*

Catalina: You love Berinthia?
  And yet you wish Antonio may be crown'd
  With happiness in his love. He loves Berinthia,
  Beyond expression. Did your eyes
  Empty their beams so much in admiration
  Of your Berinthia's beauty, you left none
  To observe your own abuses? Saw you not
  How many flames he shot into her eyes
  When they were parting, for which she paid back
  Her subtle tears? He wrung her by the hand,
  Seem'd with the greatness of his passion
  To have been overborne. Oh, cunning treachery!
  Worthy our justice. True, he commended me;
  But could you see the fountain that sent forth
  So many cozening streams, you would say Styx
  Were crystal to it. And was't not to the count,
  Whom he supposed was in pursuit of me,
  Nay, whom he knew did love me, that he might
  Fire him the more to consummate my marriage,
  That, I disposed of, he might have access
  To his beloved Berinthia, the end
  Of his desires? I can confirm it; he pray'd
  To be so happy, with my father's leave,
  To be her amorous servant, which he nobly
  Denied, partly expressing your engagements;
  If you have least suspicion of this truth—
  But do you think she loves you?
  Alas, I pity you, and the more because
  I see your troubles so amaze your judgment.
  I'll tell you my opinion, sir, o' the sudden;
  For him, he is not worth your anger;

Only thus, you shall discover to my father
She promis'd you her love; be confident
To say you did exchange faith to her; this alone
May chance assure her, and if not, I have it—
Steal her away; your love, I see, is honorable.
So much I suffer when desert is wounded,
You shall have my assistance—you apprehend me?
Keep smooth your face, and still maintain your worship
With Berinthia; things must be manag'd
And struck in the maturity, noble sir; I wish
You only fortunate in Berinthia's love.

The New Inn

Ben Jonson   *Act III, scene ii; Serio-Comic*

Lady Frampul: Oh speak and speak forever! Let mine ear
   Be feasted still, and filled with this banquet!
   No sense can ever surfeit on such truth!
   It is the marrow of all lovers' tenets!
   Who hath read Plato, Helidore, or Tatius,
   Sidney, d'Urfe, or all Love's fathers, like him?
   He is there the master of the sentences,
   Their school, their commentary, text and gloss,
   And breathes the true divinity of Love! . . .
   What penance shall I do to be received
   And reconciled to the church of Love?
   Go on procession, barefoot, to his image,
   And say some hundred penitential verses,
   There, out of Chaucer's Troilus and Criseyde?
   Or to his mother's shrine, vow a wax candle
   As large as the town maypole is, and pay it!
   Enjoin me anything this Court thinks fit.
   For I have trespassed, and blasphemed Love.
   I have indeed despised his deity,
   Whom (till this miracle wrought on me) I knew not.
   Now I adore Love, and would kiss the rushes
   That bear this reverend gentleman, his priest,
   If that would expiate—but, I fear it will not.
   For, tho' he be somewhat struck in years, and old
   Enough to be my father, he is wise,
   And only wise men love, the other covet.
   I could begin to be in love with him,
   But will not tell him yet, because I hope
   To enjoy the other hour with more delight,
   And prove him farther.
   How swift is time, and slyly steals away

From them would hug it, value it, embrace it!
I should have thought it scarce had run ten minutes,
When the whole hour is fled. Here, take your kiss, sir,
Which I most willing tender you, in Court. And I could wish
It had been twenty.

The Obstinate Lady

Sir Aston Cokain   *Act II, scene ii; Serio-Comic*

Cleanthe: Imperious love, that hatest whom thou woundest,
And those thou lovest best dost let alone!
If my obsequious duty unto thee
Can move thee to commiseration,
Instruct me how to win him, and when I
Disclose myself, assist a wretched women,
For it is in thy power to work my bliss.
He dotes upon a lady that regards
None of those miseries he undergoes
By languishing for her. With one fair stroke
Thy ignominy redeem! thou are call'd blind
Because how thou dost shoot thou dost not mind.
But what avails it me thus to implore
Or rather to reiterate those deep wishes?
Millions of hours can witness I have said,
And yet find no help! Ah! dear and ever
Most lov'd Carionil, would'st though wert so
Strongly inflam'd as I, or didst conceive,
Truly didst know, what misery lies her!
I think, though thou hadst sucked a ravenous wolf,
It would overcome thy nature, and thereby
Transform my sorrow to felicity!

The Obstinate Lady

Sir Aston Cokain   *Act II, scene i; Serio-Comic*

Cleanthe: Oh my dear lord! Brave young Carionil!
    I'll wash thy wound with my tears, stop it with sighs!
    Unkindest day that ever wore the sun!
    Thou art accursed, for giving light unto
    His hand to guide it to an act so much
    Beneath his manhood. O me! I am undone!
    What now will my disguise avail me in,
    Foolish sister Lucora? Oh ye heavens!
    Where lies our difference? Are we not the same
    By birth on both sides?—of one sex? Sure, Nature
    Degenerates against itself, or this
    Untimely—O ye gods! I dare not name it,
    Nor will I believe it. He is alive!
    So suddenly the world cannot be ruined;
    Which is if he be lost. All virtue gone—
    All valor, piety, and everything
    Mortality can boast of. My lord! noble
    Carionil! He doth not hear me. Alas!
    I am for ever the most desolate of women.
    Injurious heart strings, break! Why do you tie
    Me to a life millions of degrees more loathsome
    Than the forgetful sepulcher of death?
    Would some commiserating benevolent star
    Which carries fate in't, would, in pity to
    My misery, take me from it! For love, he
    Lies here, this bemoaned spectacle, and shall
    My passion be undervalued? Tears, nor sighs,
    Nor dirges sung by me eternally
    Can parallel our loves at full. It must be
    The same way, and it shall; The same blade
    Shall be the instrument, and I receive it

Tragediously here on my knees. Would some
Kind body would inter us in one tomb!
Be firm, my hand, and bold.

The Obstinate Lady

Sir Aston Cokain   *Act IV, scene iii; Serio-Comic*

Lucora: Stay a little.
  How frail is any woman's resolution!
  I, that so seriously have often thought
  Never to change my name, am now become
  A slave unto a Moor! I feel the mighty
  Fabric of all my maiden virtue totter.
  What can befall me worse? But I may as well
  Withstand a volley of shot, and as easily,
  As resist these new desires. 'Tis very strange
  That I, who have denied the earnest suit
  Of so complete a gentleman as was
  Carionil, and neglected his friend—
  For I will rather steal away, and do
  Mean services to my inferiors
  Than be his wife—should dote upon a person
  Some ladies scarce dare look upon—
  A Moor, A sunburnt Moor I'm utter stranger to!
  What would my father say if he should know
  My thoughts? Banish me ever from his sight,
  And never more think of Lucora's name.
  But love is not confin'd to the opinion
  Of others. Oh, this is a revenge for my
  Slighting of brave Carionil; yet, if
  He were alive again, I could not love him.
  Alas, I am undone! O that my fates
  Had been so kind as to have wrought my heart
  Fit and propense to have requited him!
  Befall what will, I am resolv'd.
  Affection that doth tend
  Not crookedly, but to a noble end,
  Is worthy; and they stubbornly repine
  At their creation who from it decline.

The Projectors

John Wilson   *Act III, scene i; Serio-Comic*

Mrs. Godsgood: Come, neighbors! I think it were not amiss if
we agreed among ourselves what we would have before the
men come! Then, in obedience to your commands, and may
this present meeting be happy and prosperous to ourselves
and the whole commonwealth of women, and that we propose those things that may be for the common good and dig-
nity of the sex. You cannot be ignorant how much your
husbands have encroached upon you, or, to speak truth, how
much we have all lost by letting the men engross all business
to themselves, without so much as asking our advice, as if we,
forsooth, were no part of them, and made to no other end
but to sit at home and prick our fingers. . . . Pray, sisters, has
not every pitiful corporation its counsel, the meanest parish
its vestry, and our very fumblers their common hall? And
shall women only lose their privilege?—shall we alone do
nothing? . . . Pray, no interruptions in the middle of a speech;
there will be time enough for all! Nor would I set up a new
thing—only revive an ancient and laudable, though somewhat antiquated, custom. I have heard of an old emperor,
somewhere or other, that ordain'd that, as he had his council
of men, so his wife should have hers of women, which should
be independent, and without appeal to t'other! . . . This
council, as I told you, whether in jest or earnest it matters
not, they call'd the She Senate; and this is that which our present interest should prick us forward to restore! Nor let it be
any rub in the way that women are forbid to speak in public,
that being meant of a congregation of men, and I speak only
of a congregation of women; for otherwise, if we were ever to
hold our tongues, to what use were they given us? Those
tongues, I say, that if they might would speak sense as well as
their own, and upon a good occasion could be as loud! Think

you, I warrant, they were given us to no other end but to lick our teeth and cheapen eggs? I think not! And why should we not use 'em, then? No doubt but we may, and perhaps, too, to as much purpose as the men; for could we look into their councils, 'tis ten to one but we should find many things ourselves would have been asham'd of! How common is it with them to be five days in wording the question, and as many more e'er they can put it right, and perhaps at last make nothing of it; whereas we are plain downright—we think what we please, and speak what we think! How does this consultation thwart that, a third both, a fourth all, as if they met only to justify the proverb, so many men, so many minds; whereas we, if the reins were in our hands, if we did not manage them better, I am sure it could not be worse!

The Roaring Girl

Thomas Dekker and Thomas Middleton

Act III, scene ii; Serio-Comic

Mrs. Gallipot: Now, Master Laxton, show your head; what news
from you? Would any husband suspect that a woman crying
"Buy any scurvy-grass," should bring love letters amongst her
herbs to his wife? Pretty trick! Fine conveyance! Had jealousy
a thousand eyes, a silly woman with scurvy-grass blinds them
all.
Laxton, with bays
Crown I thy wit for this, it deserves praise.
This makes me affect thee more, this proves thee wise.
'Lack, what poor shift is love forced to devise!
To th' point [She reads the letter]
"O sweet creature"—a sweet beginning!—"pardon my long
absence, for though shalt shortly be possessed with my presence: though Demophon was false to Phyllis, I will be to thee
as Pan-da-rus was to Cres-sida; though Aeneas make an ass of
Dido, I will die to thee ere I do so. O sweetest creature, make
much of me, for no man beneath the silver moon shall make
more of a woman than I do of thee. Furnish me therefore with
thirty pounds; you must do it of necessity for me; I languish
till I see some comfort come from thee. Protesting not to die
in thy debt, but rather to live, so as hitherto I have and will,
    Thy true Laxton ever."
Alas, poor gentleman! troth, I pity him.
How shall I raise this money? Thirty pound!
'Tis thirty sure, a 3 before an o;
I know his threes too well. My childbed linen,
Shall I pawn that for him? Then if my mark
Be known, I am undone; it may be thought
My husband's bankrupt. Which way shall I turn?
Laxton, what with my own fears and thy wants,
I'm like a needle twist two adamants.

The Roaring Girl

Thomas Dekker & Thomas Middleton

Moll: Thou'rt one of those
That thinks each woman thy fond flexible whore;
If she but cast a liberal eye upon thee,
Turn back her head, she's thine; or amongst company
By chance drink first to thee, then she's quite gone,
There is no means to help her; nay, for a need,
Wilt swear unto thy credulous fellow-lechers,
That thou art more in favor with a lady
At first sight than her monkey all her lifetime.
How many of our sex, by such as thou,
Have their good thoughts paid with a blasted name
That never deserved loosely, or did trip
In path of whoredom beyond cup and lip.
But for the stain of conscience and soul,
Better had women fall into the hands
Of an act silent than a bragging nothing;
There is no mercy in't. What durst move you, sir,
To think me whorish? A name which I'd tear out
From the high German's throat if it were lying there
To dispatch privy slanders against me.
In thee I defy all men, their worst hates
And their best flatteries, all their golden witchcrafts,
With which they entangle the poor spirits of fools,
Distressed needlewomen and trade-fallen wives;
Fish that must needs bite or themselves be bitten.
Such hungry things as these may soon be took
With a worm fastened on a golden hook.
Those are the lecher's food, his prey; he watches
For quarreling wives, and poor shifting sisters;
'Tis the best fish he takes. But why, good fisherman,
Am I thought meat for you, that never yet

Had angling rod cast towards me? 'Cause you'll say,
I'm given to sport, I'm often merry, jest.
Had mirth no kindred in the world but lust,
Oh, shame take all her friends then! But howe'er
Thou and the baser world censure my life,
I'll send 'em word by thee, and write so much
Upon thy breast, 'cause thou shalt bear in mind,
Tell them 'twere base to yield where I have conquered;
I scorn to prostitute myself to a man,
I that can prostitute a man to me;
And so I greet thee.

The Silent Woman, or Epicoene

Ben Jonson   *Act III, scene i; Serio-Comic*

Mistress Otter: By that light, I'll ha' you chained up with your
bull-dogs and bear-dogs, if you be not civil the sooner. I'll
send you to the kennel, i' faith. You were best bait me with
your bull, bear, and horse! Never a time that the courtiers or
collegiates come to the house, but you make it a Shrove
Tuesday! I would have you get your Whitsuntide velvet cap
and your staff i' your hand to entertain 'em; yes, in troth, do
. . . Is a bear a fit beast, or a bull, to mix in society with great
ladies? By my integrity, I'll send you over to the Bankside, I'll
commit you to the master of the Garden, if I hear but a sylla-
ble more. Must my house, or my roof, be polluted with the
scent of bears and bulls, when it is perfumed for great ladies?
Is this according to the instrument when I married you? That
I would be princess and reign in mine own house, and you
would be my subject and obey me? What did you bring me,
should make you thus peremptory? Do I allow you half-
crown a day to spend where you will among your gamesters,
to vex and torment me at such times as these? Who gives you
your horse-meat and man's meat? Your three suits of apparel a
year? Your four pair of stockings, one silk, three worsted?
Your clean linen, your bands and cuffs, when I can get you to
wear 'em? Tis mar'l you ha' 'em on now. Who graces you
with courtiers or great personages, to speak to you out of
their coaches and come home to your house. Were you ever
so much as looked upon by a lord, or a lady, before I married
you, but on the Easter or Whitsun holidays, and then out at
the Banqueting House window, when Ned Whiting or
George Stone were at the stake? Answer me to that. And did
not I take you up from thence in an old greasy buff-doublet,
with points, and green velvet sleeves out at the elbows? You
forget this. Oh, here are some o' the gallants. Go to, behave

yourself distinctly, and with good morality, or I protest, I'll take away your exhibition.

Bibliography

Abdelazer, or, The Moor's Revenge
Aphra Behn

> *Aphra Behn: Five Plays* Introduction by Maureen Duffy
> London: Methuen London Ltd. 1990

Adventures of Five Hours
Sir Samuel Tuke

> *A Select Collection of Old English Plays, Vol.* 15 edited by Robert
> Dodsley, originally published in 1744

All Mistaken, or, The Mad Couple
James Howard

> *A Select Collection of Old English Plays, Vol.* 15 edited by Robert
> Dodsley, originally published in 1744

The Beaux' Stratagem
George Farquhar

> *The Beaux' Stratagem* edited by Michael Cordner; London:
> Ernest Benn Ltd./New York: W.W. Morrow 1976

> *The Beaux' Stratagem* edited by Charles N. Fifer; Lincoln:
> University of Nebraska Press 1977

> *The Beaux' Stratagem* edited by A. Norman Jeffares;
> Edinburgh: Oliver and Boyd 1972

> *Complete Works of George Farquhar, Vol.* 2 edited by Charles
> Stonehill; New York: The Gordian Press, 1967/London: The
> Nonesuch Press, 1930

> *The Works of George Farquhar* edited by Shirley Strum Kenny;
> Oxford: The Clarendon Press 1988

The Changeling
Thomas Middleton and William Rowley

> *The Changeling* edited by Joost Daalder; London: A.C. Black
> New York: W.W. Norton 1990

> *The Changeling* edited by George Walton Williams; Lincoln:
> The University of Nebraska Press 1966

> *The Changeling* edited by Matthew W. Black; Philadelphia:
> University of Pennsylvania Press 1966

> *Drama of the English Renaissance Vol. 2: The Stuart Period* edit-
> ed by Russell A. Fraser and Norman Rabkin; New York:
> Macmillan Publishing Co./London: Collier Macmillan
> Publishers 1976

The Conscious Lovers
Richard Steele

> *Six Eighteenth Century* edited by John Harold Wilson; Boston:
> Houghton Mifflin Co./ Cambridge: The Riverside Press 1963

> *The Conscious Lovers* edited by Shirley Strum Kenny; Lincoln:
> University of Nebraska Press 1968

> *The Plays of Richard Steele* edited by Shirley Strum Kenny
> Oxford: The Clarendon Press 1971

The Constant Couple
George Farquhar

> *The Constant Couple;* London: Methuen Drama 1988

> *The Works of George Farquhar* edited by Shirley Strum Kenny;
> Oxford: The Clarendon Press 1988

> *The Complete Works of George Farquhar* edited by Charles
> Stonehill; New York: The Gordian Press 1967/London: The
> Nonesuch Press 1930

The Contrast
Royall Tyler

> *The Contrast;* New York: AMS Press 1970

The Country Wife
William Wycherley

Plays of William Wycherley edited by Peter Holland; Cambridge: Cambridge University Press 1981

Complete Plays of Wycherley edited by Gerald Weales; New York: New York University Press 1967

The Plays of William Wycherley edited by Arthur Friedman; Oxford: Clarendon Press 1979

The Complete Works of William Wycherley edited by Montague Summers; New York: Russell and Russell Inc. 1964

Signet Classic Book of Restoration Drama edited by Ronald Berham; New York: New American Library 1980

The Country Wife edited by James Ogden; New York: W.W. Norton 1991

The Country Wife edited by David Cook and John Swannell; London: Methuen 1975

The Country Wife edited by John Dixon Hunt; London: Ernest Benn Ltd. 1973

The Country Wife edited by Thomas H. Fujimura; Lincoln: University of Nebraska Press 1965

Three Restoration Plays edited by Gamini Salgado; Baltimore: Penguin 1968

The Country Wit
John Crowne

The Comedies of John Crowne edited by B.J. McMullin; New York: Garland Publishing Inc. 1984

Dramatic Works of John Crowne, Vol. 3; Edinburgh: 1874/New York: Benjamin Blom, 1967

Cutter of Coleman Street
Abraham Cowley

Essays and Plays of Abraham Cowley edited by A.R. Waller; Cambridge University Press 1906

Cutter of Coleman Street edited by Darlene Johnson Gravett;
Garland Publishing Inc. New York, London 1987

The Destruction of Jerusalem, Part 1
John Crowne

> *Dramatic Works of John Crowne, Vol.* 2; Edinburgh 1874,
> Benjamin Blom, New York 1967

The Distress'd Wife
John Gay

> *Dramatic Works of John Gay* edited by John Fuller; Clarendon
> Press, Oxford 1983

Don Sebastian
John Dryden

> *The Works of John Dryden, Vol.* 15 Editor, Earl Miner;
> University of California Press Berkeley, LA, London, 1976
>
> *Dryden: The Dramatic Works* edited by Montague Summers;
> Nonesuch Press, London 1932
>
> *Four Tragedies* edited by L.A. Beaurline and Fredson Bowers;
> Chicago: University of Chicago Press 1967
>
> *John Dryden, Vol.* 2 edited by George Saintsbury; New York:
> A.A. Wyn Inc. 1950

The Double Dealer
William Congreve

> *The Double Dealer* edited by J.C. Ross; W.W. Norton, New
> York/Ernest Benn Ltd., London 1981
>
> *Comedies of William Congreve* edited by Anthony G.
> Henderson; Cambridge University Press 1982
>
> *Complete Plays of William Congreve* edited by Herbert Davis;
> University of Chicago Press Chicago, London 1967
>
> *Comedies by Congreve* edited by Bonamy Dobree; Oxford
> University Press, London 1959

Complete Works of William Congreve, Vol. 2 edited by
Montague Summers; Russell and Russell Inc., New York 1964

The Dutch Courtesan
John Marston

> *Selected Plays of John Marston* edited by MacDonald P. Jackson,
> Michael Neill; Cambridge University Press Cambridge 1986
>
> *Plays by John Marston, Vol.* 2 edited by H. Harvey Wood;
> Oliver and Boyd Edinburgh, London 1938
>
> *The Dutch Courtesan* edited by Peter Davison; University of
> California Press Berkeley, LA 1968
>
> *The Works of John Marston* edited by A.H. Bullen; John C.
> Nimmo, London 1888
>
> *Drama of the English Renaissance Vol 2: The Stuart Period* edited
> by Russell A. Fraser and Norman Rabkin; Macmillan
> Publishing Co., New York/Collier Macmillan Publishers,
> London 1976
>
> *The Dutch Courtesan* edited by M.L. Wine; University of
> Nebraska Press Lincoln 1965

Epicoene, or, The Silent Woman
Ben Jonson

> edited by R.V. Holdsworth; Ernest Benn Ltd, London/WW
> Norton, New York 1979
>
> Methuen London Heinemann, Portsmouth 1989
>
> *Epicoene* edited by Edward Partridge; Yale University Press
> New Haven, London 1971
>
> *Epicoene, or, The Silent Woman* edited by L.A. Beaurline;
> Lincoln: University of Nebraska Press 1966
>
> *Selected Plays of Ben Jonson* edited by Johanna Proctor;
> Cambridge University Press Cambridge, New York 1989
>
> *The Complete Plays of Ben Jonson* edited by G.A. Wilkes, based
> on the edition edited by C.H. Herford and Evelyn Simpson;
> Clarendon Press (OUP) Oxford, New York 1981

The Example
James Shirley

> *The Dramatic Works and Poems of Shirley, Vol.* 3 edited by
> William Gifford and Alexander Dyce; John Murray, London
> 1833
>
> *The Example: An Old Spelling Critical Edition,* edited by
> William F. Jones; Garland Publishing Inc., New York, London
> 1987

The Fair Penitent
Nicholas Rowe

> *The Fair Penitent,* edited by Malcolm Goldstein; University of
> Nebraska Press Lincoln 1969
>
> *Six Eighteenth Century Plays* edited by John Harold Wilson;
> Houghton Mifflin, Boston Riverside Press, Cambridge
> Riverside Editions, general editor, Gordon N. Ray
>
> *Plays of the Restoration and Eighteenth Century* edited by
> Dougald MacMillan and Howard Mumford Jones; New York:
> Henry Holt and Company 1931

Fatal Curiosity
George Lillo

> *Fatal Curiosity* edited by William H. McBurney; Lincoln:
> University of Nebraska Press 1966

Gallathea
John Lyly

> *Drama of the English Renaissance Vol.* 1: *The Tudor Period* edited
> by Russell A. Fraser and Norman Rabkin; Macmillan
> Publishing Co., NY/Collier Macmillan Publishers, London
> 1976
>
> *Gallathea and Midas* edited by Anne Begor Lancashire;
> Lincoln: University of Nebraska Press 1969

The Guardian
Abraham Cowley

> *Essays and Plays of Abraham Cowley* edited by A.R. Waller;
> Cambridge: Cambridge University Press 1906

> *The Complete Works in Verse and Prose of Abraham Cowley* edit-
> ed by Alexander B. Grosart; New York: AMS Press Inc 1967

Hyde Park
James Shirley

> *Drama of the English Renaissance Vol. 2: The Stuart Period* edit-
> ed by Russell A. Fraser and Norman Rabkin; New York:
> Macmillan Publishing Co./London: Collier Macmillan
> Publishers 1976

> *Hyde Park* Methuen London 1987

> *The Dramatic Works and Poems of James Shirley, Vol.* 2 edited by
> William Gifford and Alexander Dyce; London: John Murray
> 1833

I'll Tell You What
Elizabeth Inchbald

> *Selected Comedies* edited by Roger Manvell; University Press of
> America, Inc. Lanham (NY), London 1987

King Henry V, or, The Conquest of France
Aaron Hill

> *The Plays of Aaron Hill* edited by Calhoun Winton; New York:
> Garland Publishing Inc. 1981

The Libertine
Thomas Shadwell

> *The Complete Works of Thomas Shadwell* edited by Montague
> Summers; London: The Fortune Press 1927

The Lost Lady
William Barclay

> *A Select Collection of Old English Plays,* Volume 12 edited by
> Robert Dodsley 1744

The London Merchant
George Lillo

> *The London Merchant* edited by William H. McBurney;
> University of Nebraska Press, Lincoln 1965
>
> *Six Eighteenth Century Plays* edited by John Harold Wilson;
> Boston: Houghton Mifflin/Cambridge: The Riverside Press
> 1963
>
> *British Dramatists from Dryden to Sheridan* edited by George
> H. Nettleton and Arthur E. Case; Boston: Houghton Mifflin
> Co./Cambridge: Riverside Press 1939
>
> *Plays of the Restoration and Eighteenth Century* edited by
> Dougald MacMillan and Howard Mumford Jones; New York:
> Henry Holt and Company 1931

Love Tricks
James Shirley

> *The Dramatic Works of Shirley, Vol.* 1 edited by William Gifford
> and Alexander Dyce; John Murray, London 1833

Madam Fickle
Thomas Durfey

> *Two Comedies by Thomas D'Urfey* edited by Jack A. Vaughn;
> Cranbury (NJ), London: Associated University Presses, Inc.
> 1976

The Maid's Revenge
James Shirley

> *The Dramatic Works of Shirley, Vol.* 1 edited by William Gifford
> and Alexander Dyce; London: John Murray 1833

The Man of Mode
George Etherege

>   *The Man of Mode;* London: Methuen London Ltd 1988
>
>   *The Man of Mode* edited by John Barnard; London: Ernest Benn Ltd./New York: W.W. Norton and Co. Inc 1979
>
>   *The Man of Mode* edited by W.B. Carnochan; Lincoln: University of Nebraska 1966
>
>   *The Plays of Sir George Etherege* edited by Michael Cordner; Cambridge: Cambridge University Press 1982

The Mourning Bride
William Congreve

>   *The Complete Works of William Congreve, Vol.* 2 edited by Montague Summers; New York: Russell and Russell Inc. 1964
>
>   *Complete Plays of William Congreve* edited by Herbert Davis; Chicago: University of Chicago Press 1967

The New Inn
Ben Jonson

>   *The New Inn;* London: Methuen London Ltd. 1987
>
>   *Selected Plays of Ben Jonson* edited by Johanna Proctor; Cambridge: Cambridge University Press 1989
>
>   *The Complete Plays of Ben Jonson, Vol.* 4 edited by G.A. Wilkes, based on the edition edited by C.H. Herford and Evelyn Simpson; Oxford: Clarendon Press 1981

A New Way to Pay Old Debts
Philip Massinger

>   *Plays of Philip Massinger* edited by Arthur Symons; London: Vizetelly & Co. 1887
>
>   *The Poems and Plays of Philip Massinger* edited by Philip Edwards and Colin Gibson; Oxford: Clarendon Press 1976
>
>   *A New Way to Pay Old Debts;* London: Methuen London Ltd. 1983

A New Way to Pay Old Debts edited by T.W. Craik; London: Ernest Benn Ltd. 1964

A New Way to Pay Old Debts edited by M. St. Clare Byrne; London: University of London, Athlone Press 1956

Selected Plays of Philip Massinger edited by Colin Gibson; Cambridge: Cambridge University Press 1978

The Obstinate Lady
Sir Aston Cokain

> *The Obstinate Lady* edited by Catherine M. Shaw; Garland Publishing Inc. New York, London 1986
>
> *The Dramatic Works of Sir Aston Cokain* edited by James Maidment and W.H. Logan; Edinburgh: 1874/New York: Benjamin Blom 1967

Perkin Warbeck
John Ford

> *Perkin Warbeck* edited by Donald K. Anderson Jr.; Lincoln: University of Nebraska Press 1965
>
> *Perkin Warbeck* edited by Peter Ure; London: Methuen & Co. 1968
>
> *Selected Plays of John Ford* edited by Colin Gibson; Cambridge: Cambridge University Press 1986

Polly Honeycombe
George Colman

> *Eighteenth Century Afterpieces* edited by Richard W. Bevis; Oxford: Oxford University Press 1970

The Projectors
John Wilson

> *The Dramatic Works of John Wilson* edited by James Maidment and W.H. Logan; Edinburgh: 1874/New York: Benjamin Blom 1967

The Provoked Wife
Sir John Vanbrugh

> *The Provoked Wife* edited by James L. Smith; London: Ernest Benn Ltd. 1974
>
> *The Provoked Wife* edited by Curt A. Zimansky; Lincoln: University of Nebraska Press 1969
>
> *Sir John Vanbrugh, Vol.* 1 edited by W.C. Ward; London: Lawrence and Bullen 1893
>
> *British Plays from the Restoration to* 1820 edited by Montrose J. Moses; Boston: Little Brown and Co. 1931

The Rebellion
Thomas Rawlins

> *A Select Collection of Old English Plays, Vol.* 14 edited by Robert Dodsley, originally published in 1744

The Relapse
Sir John Vanbrugh

> *The Relapse* edited by Curt A. Zimansky; Lincoln: University of Nebraska Press 1970
>
> *The Relapse* edited by Bernard Harris; London: Ernest Benn Ltd. 1971
>
> *British Dramatists from Dryden to Sheridan* edited by George H. Nettleton and Arthur E. Case; Boston: Houghton Mifflin Co. 1939
>
> *Sir John Vanbrugh, Vol.* 1 edited by W.C. Ward; London: Lawrence and Bullen 1893

The Revenger's Tragedy
Cyril Tourneur

> *The Revenger's Tragedy;* London: Methuen London Ltd. 1987
>
> *The Revenger's Tragedy* edited by Brian Gibbons; London: Ernest Benn Ltd. 1967
>
> *The Revenger's Tragedy* edited by Lawrence J. Ross; Lincoln: University of Nebraska Press 1966

The Revenger's Tragedy edited by R. A. Foakes; Cambridge: Harvard University Press 1966

Webster and Tourneur: Four Plays edited by John Addington Symonds; New York: Hill and Wang 1956

The Rivals
Richard Brinsley Sheridan

Dramatic Works of Richard Brinsley Sheridan edited by Cecil Price; London: Oxford University Press 1973

Sheridan: Plays edited by Cecil Price; London: Oxford University Press 1975

Plays and Poems of Richard Brinsley Sheridan, Vol. 1 edited by R. Crompton Rhodes; New York: The Macmillan Company 1929

The Rivals edited by Elizabeth Duthie; London: Ernest Benn Ltd./New York: W.W. Norton and Co. Inc. 1979

The Roaring Girl
Thomas Dekker and Thomas Middleton

Drama of the English Renaissance Vol. 2: *The Stuart Period* edited by Russell A. Fraser and Norman Rabkin; New York: Macmillan Publishing Company/London: Collier Macmillan Publishers 1976

The Roaring Girl edited by Ander Gomme; London: Ernest Benn Ltd./New York: W.W. Norton and Co., Inc. 1976

The Rover
Aphra Behn

Aphra Behn: Five Plays Introduction by Maureen Duffy; London: Methuen London Ltd. 1990

The Rover, London: Methuen London Ltd. 1986, 1987

The Rover edited by Frederick M. Link; Lincoln: University of Nebraska Press 1967

The Sack of Rome
Mercy Otis Warren

> *The Plays and Poems of Mercy Otis Warren* edited by Benjamin
> Franklin V; Delmar (NY): Scholar's Facsimiles and Reprints

She Would and She Would Not
Colley Cibber

> *The Plays of Colley Cibber, Vol.* 1 edited by Rodney L. Hayley;
> New York: Garland Publishing Company 1980

Simplicity
Lady Mary Worley Montague

> *Essays, Poems, and Simplicity—A Comedy* edited by Robert
> Halsband and Isobel Grundy; Oxford: The Clarendon Press
> 1977

Three Weeks After Marriage
Samuel Foote

> *Plays by Samuel Foote and Arthur Murphy* edited by George
> Taylor; Cambridge: Cambridge University Press 1984

'Tis Pity She's A Whore
John Ford

> *'Tis Pity She's a Whore* edited by N.W. Bawcutt; Lincoln:
> University of Nebraska Press 1966

> *'Tis Pity She's a Whore* edited by Brian Morris; London: Ernest
> Benn Ltd. 1968

> *Selected Plays of John Ford* edited by Colin Gibson; Cambridge:
> Cambridge University Press 1986

> *Drama of the English Renaissance, Vol. 2: The Stuart Period* edit-
> ed by Russell A. Fraser and Norman Rabkin; New York:
> Macmillan Publishing Company/London: Collier Macmillan
> Publishers 1976

Two Noble Kinsmen
William Shakespeare & John Fletcher

Beaumont & Fletcher: Dramatic Works, Vol. 7 edited by Fredson Bowers; Cambridge: Cambridge University Press 1989

The Two Noble Kinsmen edited by Eugene M. Waith; Oxford: The Clarendon Press/New York: Oxford University Press 1989

The Two Noble Kinsmen edited by Clifford Leech; New York: New American Library 1966

The Two Noble Kinsmen; London: Methuen London Ltd 1986

The Way of the World
William Congreve

The Way of the World edited by Kathleen Martha Lynch; Lincoln: University of Nebraska Press 1965

The Way of the World edited by Brian Gibbons; London: Ernest Benn Ltd. 1971

Comedies of William Congreve edited by Anthony G. Henderson; Cambridge University Press 1982

Complete Plays of William Congreve edited by Herbert Davis; University of Chicago Press Chicago, London 1967

Comedies by Congreve edited by Bonamy Dobree; Oxford University Press, London 1959

Complete Works of William Congreve, Vol. 3 edited by Montague Summers; Russell and Russell Inc., New York 1964

British Dramatists from Dryden to Sheridan edited by George H. Nettleton and Arthur E. Case; Boston: Houghton Mifflin Co. 1939

British Plays from the Restoration to 1820 edited by Montrose J. Moses; Boston: Little Brown and Co. 1931

The Way to Keep Him
Arthur Murphy

Eighteenth Century Afterpieces edited by Richard W. Bevis; Oxford: Oxford University Press 1970

The White Devil
John Webster

The White Devil edited by F.L. Lucas; New York: Macmillan Publishing Company 1959

The White Devil edited by John Russell Brown; Cambridge: Harvard University Press 1960

The White Devil edited by Elizabeth M. Brennan; London: Ernest Benn Ltd. 1966

The White Devil edited by Clive Hart; Berkeley: University of California Press 1970

Selected Plays of John Webster edited by Jonathan Dollimore and Alan Sinfield; Cambridge: Cambridge University Press 1983

Webster and Tourneur: Four Plays edited by John Addington Symonds; New York: Hill and Wang 1956

The Complete Works of John Webster, Vol. 1 edited by F.L. Lucas; London: Chatto and Windus 1927

The Witch of Edmonton
Thomas Dekker, John Ford, William Rowley

The Witch of Edmonton Commentary by Simon Trussler Notes by Jacqui Russell; London: Methuen London Ltd. 1983

The Dramatic Works of Thomas Dekker edited by Fredson Bowers; Cambridge: Cambridge University Press 1958

Thomas Dekker edited by Ernest Rhys; London: Ernest Benn Ltd. 1949